I0616443

Organizing My Thoughts

Manifesting My Goals

2026

A Journal for Reflection, Planning, and Achievement
Black-and-White Edition

ORGANIZING MY THOUGHTS, MANIFESTING MY GOALS 2026

ISBN: 978-1-967592-25-8
Published by GrantWatch, Inc.
Boynton Beach, Florida
For information, contact:
support@grantwatch.com

A new year brings goals and the
opportunity for progress and achievement.

What we choose to manifest matters.

If we manifest trying, we spend the year trying.

If we manifest achievement, we move with intention
toward what we want to accomplish.

Have faith in what you are capable of and in yourself.

Now take the time to
reflect, plan, progress, and achieve in 2026.

Be grateful for every achievement, large and small.

Libby Hikind

ORGANIZING MY THOUGHTS, MANIFESTING MY GOALS 2026

2026 Calendar

ORGANIZING MY THOUGHTS, MANIFESTING MY GOALS 2026

January

S	M	T	W	T	F	S
				1	2	3
4	5	6	7	8	9	10
11	12	13	14	15	16	17
18	19	20	21	22	23	24
25	26	27	28	29	30	31

February

S	M	T	W	T	F	S
1	2	3	4	5	6	7
8	9	10	11	12	13	14
15	16	17	18	19	20	21
22	23	24	25	26	27	28

March

S	M	T	W	T	F	S
1	2	3	4	5	6	7
8	9	10	11	12	13	14
15	16	17	18	19	20	21
22	23	24	25	26	27	28
29	30	31				

April

S	M	T	W	T	F	S
			1	2	3	4
5	6	7	8	9	10	11
12	13	14	15	16	17	18
19	20	21	22	23	24	25
26	27	28	29	30		

May

S	M	T	W	T	F	S
					1	2
3	4	5	6	7	8	9
10	11	12	13	14	15	16
17	18	19	20	21	22	23
24/31	25	26	27	28	29	30

June

S	M	T	W	T	F	S
	1	2	3	4	5	6
7	8	9	10	11	12	13
14	15	16	17	18	19	20
21	22	23	24	25	26	27
28	29	30				

July

S	M	T	W	T	F	S
			1	2	3	4
5	6	7	8	9	10	11
12	13	14	15	16	17	18
19	20	21	22	23	24	25
26	27	28	29	30	31	

August

S	M	T	W	T	F	S
						1
2	3	4	5	6	7	8
9	10	11	12	13	14	15
16	17	18	19	20	21	22
23/30	24/31	25	26	27	28	29

September

S	M	T	W	T	F	S
		1	2	3	4	5
6	7	8	9	10	11	12
13	14	15	16	17	18	19
20	21	22	23	24	25	26
27	28	29	30			

October

S	M	T	W	T	F	S
				1	2	3
4	5	6	7	8	9	10
11	12	13	14	15	16	17
18	19	20	21	22	23	24
25	26	27	28	29	30	31

November

S	M	T	W	T	F	S
1	2	3	4	5	6	7
8	9	10	11	12	13	14
15	16	17	18	19	20	21
22	23	24	25	26	27	28
29	30					

December

S	M	T	W	T	F	S
		1	2	3	4	5
6	7	8	9	10	11	12
13	14	15	16	17	18	19
20	21	22	23	24	25	26
27	28	29	30	31		

What's On Your Mind?

★ _____

★ _____

★ _____

Month **JANUARY 2026**

Ideas, Tasks, Chores, Wishes, Dreams, Desires

➤ _____

➤ _____

➤ _____

➤ _____

➤ _____

➤ _____

➤ _____

➤ _____

➤ _____

➤ _____

➤ _____

➤ _____

VISION ——————— BOARD

Start each month with clarity and purpose. Reflect, plan, manifest. This journal is designed to help you stay organized, set priorities, and achieve your goals.

(Month): _____

Health

Career & Finances

Relationships & Social Life

Travel

Fitness

Spirituality & Mindfulness

Monthly goals

HEALTH GOALS

♡ _____

♡ _____

♡ _____

CAREER AND WORK GOALS

♡ _____

♡ _____

♡ _____

FITNESS GOALS

♡ _____

♡ _____

♡ _____

Monthly goals

RELATIONSHIP & SOCIAL LIFE GOALS

- ♡ _____
- ♡ _____
- ♡ _____

TRAVEL GOALS

- ♡ _____
- ♡ _____
- ♡ _____

SPIRITUAL AND MINDFULNESS GOALS

- ♡ _____
- ♡ _____
- ♡ _____

ORGANIZING MY THOUGHTS, MANIFESTING MY GOALS 2026

Monthly goals

FINANCE GOALS

♡ _____
♡ _____
♡ _____

OTHER GOALS

♡ _____
♡ _____
♡ _____

OTHER GOALS

♡ _____
♡ _____
♡ _____

ORGANIZING MY THOUGHTS, MANIFESTING MY GOALS 2026

Weekly Planner

WEEK OF :

MONTH :

MONDAY

TUESDAY

WEDNESDAY

THURSDAY

FRIDAY

SATURDAY

NOTE :

QUOTE :

ORGANIZING MY THOUGHTS, MANIFESTING MY GOALS 2026

5-minute journaling:
Today I am grateful for...

_____

_____

_____

_____

_____

_____

_____

_____

_____

_____

_____

_____

_____

_____

_____

_____

_____

_____

5-minute journaling:
Today I am grateful for...

_____

_____

_____

_____

_____

_____

_____

_____

_____

_____

_____

_____

_____

_____

_____

_____

_____

_____

_____

5-minute journaling:
Today I am grateful for...

_____

_____

_____

_____

_____

_____

_____

_____

_____

_____

_____

_____

_____

_____

_____

_____

_____

_____

Weekly Planner

WEEK OF :

MONTH :

MONDAY

TUESDAY

WEDNESDAY

THURSDAY

FRIDAY

SATURDAY

NOTE :

QUOTE :

ORGANIZING MY THOUGHTS, MANIFESTING MY GOALS 2026

5-minute journaling:
Today I am grateful for...

_____

_____

_____

_____

_____

_____

_____

_____

_____

_____

_____

_____

_____

_____

_____

_____

_____

_____

5-minute journaling:
Today I am grateful for...

_____

_____

_____

_____

_____

_____

_____

_____

_____

_____

_____

_____

_____

_____

_____

_____

_____

_____

_____

_____

_____

5-minute journaling:
Today I am grateful for...

_____

_____

_____

_____

_____

_____

_____

_____

_____

_____

_____

_____

_____

_____

_____

_____

_____

_____

_____

_____

5-minute journaling:
Today I am grateful for...

_____

_____

_____

_____

_____

_____

_____

_____

_____

_____

_____

_____

_____

_____

_____

_____

_____

_____

_____

_____

5-minute journaling:
Today I am grateful for...

_____

_____

_____

_____

_____

_____

_____

_____

_____

_____

_____

_____

_____

_____

_____

_____

_____

_____

_____

5-minute journaling:
Today I am grateful for...

_____

_____

_____

_____

_____

_____

_____

_____

_____

_____

_____

_____

_____

_____

_____

_____

_____

_____

_____

5-minute journaling:
Today I am grateful for...

_____

_____

_____

_____

_____

_____

_____

_____

_____

_____

_____

_____

_____

_____

_____

_____

_____

_____

_____

Weekly Planner

WEEK OF :

MONTH :

MONDAY

TUESDAY

WEDNESDAY

THURSDAY

FRIDAY

SATURDAY

NOTE :

QUOTE :

ORGANIZING MY THOUGHTS, MANIFESTING MY GOALS 2026

5-minute journaling:
Today I am grateful for...

_____

_____

_____

_____

_____

_____

_____

_____

_____

_____

_____

_____

_____

_____

_____

_____

_____

_____

_____

_____

_____

5-minute journaling:
Today I am grateful for...

_____

_____

_____

_____

_____

_____

_____

_____

_____

_____

_____

_____

_____

_____

_____

_____

_____

_____

_____

5-minute journaling:
Today I am grateful for...

_____

_____

_____

_____

_____

_____

_____

_____

_____

_____

_____

_____

_____

_____

_____

_____

_____

_____

_____

_____

5-minute journaling:
Today I am grateful for...

_____

_____

_____

_____

_____

_____

_____

_____

_____

_____

_____

_____

_____

_____

_____

_____

_____

_____

5-minute journaling:
Today I am grateful for...

_____

_____

_____

_____

_____

_____

_____

_____

_____

_____

_____

_____

_____

_____

_____

_____

_____

_____

5-minute journaling:
Today I am grateful for...

_____

_____

_____

_____

_____

_____

_____

_____

_____

_____

_____

_____

_____

_____

_____

_____

_____

_____

_____

5-minute journaling:
Today I am grateful for...

_____

_____

_____

_____

_____

_____

_____

_____

_____

_____

_____

_____

_____

_____

_____

_____

_____

_____

_____

Weekly Planner

WEEK OF :

MONTH :

MONDAY

TUESDAY

WEDNESDAY

THURSDAY

FRIDAY

SATURDAY

NOTE :

QUOTE :

ORGANIZING MY THOUGHTS, MANIFESTING MY GOALS 2026

5-minute journaling:
Today I am grateful for...

_____

_____

_____

_____

_____

_____

_____

_____

_____

_____

_____

_____

_____

_____

_____

_____

_____

_____

_____

_____

_____

5-minute journaling:
Today I am grateful for...

_____

_____

_____

_____

_____

_____

_____

_____

_____

_____

_____

_____

_____

_____

_____

_____

_____

_____

5-minute journaling:
Today I am grateful for...

_____

_____

_____

_____

_____

_____

_____

_____

_____

_____

_____

_____

_____

_____

_____

_____

_____

_____

_____

_____

5-minute journaling:
Today I am grateful for...

_____

_____

_____

_____

_____

_____

_____

_____

_____

_____

_____

_____

_____

_____

_____

_____

_____

_____

_____

_____

5-minute journaling:
Today I am grateful for...

_____

_____

_____

_____

_____

_____

_____

_____

_____

_____

_____

_____

_____

_____

_____

_____

_____

_____

_____

_____

5-minute journaling:
Today I am grateful for...

_____

_____

_____

_____

_____

_____

_____

_____

_____

_____

_____

_____

_____

_____

_____

_____

_____

_____

_____

_____

5-minute journaling:
Today I am grateful for...

_____

_____

_____

_____

_____

_____

_____

_____

_____

_____

_____

_____

_____

_____

_____

_____

_____

_____

_____

_____

_____

_____

Weekly Planner

WEEK OF :

MONTH :

MONDAY

TUESDAY

WEDNESDAY

THURSDAY

FRIDAY

SATURDAY

NOTE :

QUOTE :

ORGANIZING MY THOUGHTS, MANIFESTING MY GOALS 2026

5-minute journaling:
Today I am grateful for...

_____

_____

_____

_____

_____

_____

_____

_____

_____

_____

_____

_____

_____

_____

_____

_____

_____

_____

_____

5-minute journaling:
Today I am grateful for...

_____

_____

_____

_____

_____

_____

_____

_____

_____

_____

_____

_____

_____

_____

_____

_____

_____

_____

_____

_____

_____

5-minute journaling:
Today I am grateful for...

_____

_____

_____

_____

_____

_____

_____

_____

_____

_____

_____

_____

_____

_____

_____

_____

_____

_____

_____

_____

5-minute journaling:
Today I am grateful for...

_____

_____

_____

_____

_____

_____

_____

_____

_____

_____

_____

_____

_____

_____

_____

_____

_____

5-minute journaling:
Today I am grateful for...

_____

_____

_____

_____

_____

_____

_____

_____

_____

_____

_____

_____

_____

_____

_____

_____

_____

_____

_____

5-minute journaling:
Today I am grateful for...

_____

_____

_____

_____

_____

_____

_____

_____

_____

_____

_____

_____

_____

_____

_____

_____

_____

_____

5-minute journaling:
Today I am grateful for...

_____
_____
_____
_____
_____
_____
_____
_____
_____
_____
_____
_____
_____
_____
_____
_____
_____
_____
_____
_____
_____
_____
_____

MILESTONE ACCOMPLISHMENT

1) What did I accomplish:
_____

_____

2) When did I accomplish it:
_____

3) How did you accomplish it:
_____

_____

_____

4) What motivated you to accomplish it:
_____

_____

_____

5) Did you face any challenges while accomplishing it:
_____

_____

_____

6) How will you celebrate your accomplishment:
_____

_____

_____

What's On
Your Mind?

★ _____

★ _____

★ _____

Month **FEBRUARY 2026**

Ideas, Tasks, Chores, Wishes, Dreams, Desires

➤ _____

➤ _____

➤ _____

➤ _____

➤ _____

➤ _____

➤ _____

➤ _____

➤ _____

➤ _____

➤ _____

➤ _____

VISION —————— BOARD

Start each month with clarity and purpose. Reflect, plan, manifest. This journal is designed to help you stay organized, set priorities, and achieve your goals.

(Month): _____

Health

Career & Finances

Relationships & Social Life

Travel

Fitness

Spirituality & Mindfulness

ORGANIZING MY THOUGHTS, MANIFESTING MY GOALS 2026

Monthly goals

HEALTH GOALS

- ♡ _____
- ♡ _____
- ♡ _____

CAREER AND WORK GOALS

- ♡ _____
- ♡ _____
- ♡ _____

FITNESS GOALS

- ♡ _____
- ♡ _____
- ♡ _____

Monthly goals

RELATIONSHIP & SOCIAL LIFE GOALS

♡ _____

♡ _____

♡ _____

TRAVEL GOALS

♡ _____

♡ _____

♡ _____

SPIRITUAL AND MINDFULNESS GOALS

♡ _____

♡ _____

♡ _____

Monthly goals

FINANCE GOALS

♡ _____
♡ _____
♡ _____

OTHER GOALS

♡ _____
♡ _____
♡ _____

OTHER GOALS

♡ _____
♡ _____
♡ _____

Weekly Planner

WEEK OF :

MONTH :

MONDAY

TUESDAY

WEDNESDAY

THURSDAY

FRIDAY

SATURDAY

NOTE :

QUOTE :

ORGANIZING MY THOUGHTS, MANIFESTING MY GOALS 2026

5-minute journaling:
Today I am grateful for...

_____

_____

_____

_____

_____

_____

_____

_____

_____

_____

_____

_____

_____

_____

_____

_____

_____

_____

_____

_____

_____

5-minute journaling:
Today I am grateful for...

_____
_____
_____
_____
_____
_____
_____
_____
_____
_____
_____
_____
_____
_____
_____
_____
_____
_____
_____
_____

5-minute journaling:
Today I am grateful for...

_____

_____

_____

_____

_____

_____

_____

_____

_____

_____

_____

_____

_____

_____

_____

_____

_____

_____

_____

_____

_____

5-minute journaling:
Today I am grateful for...

_____

_____

_____

_____

_____

_____

_____

_____

_____

_____

_____

_____

_____

_____

_____

_____

_____

_____

_____

_____

5-minute journaling:
Today I am grateful for...

_____

_____

_____

_____

_____

_____

_____

_____

_____

_____

_____

_____

_____

_____

_____

_____

_____

_____

_____

5-minute journaling:
Today I am grateful for...

_____

_____

_____

_____

_____

_____

_____

_____

_____

_____

_____

_____

_____

_____

_____

_____

_____

_____

5-minute journaling:
Today I am grateful for...

_____

_____

_____

_____

_____

_____

_____

_____

_____

_____

_____

_____

_____

_____

_____

_____

_____

_____

_____

_____

Weekly Planner

WEEK OF :

MONTH :

MONDAY

TUESDAY

WEDNESDAY

THURSDAY

FRIDAY

SATURDAY

NOTE :

QUOTE :

ORGANIZING MY THOUGHTS, MANIFESTING MY GOALS 2026

5-minute journaling:
Today I am grateful for...

_____

_____

_____

_____

_____

_____

_____

_____

_____

_____

_____

_____

_____

_____

_____

_____

_____

_____

_____

_____

_____

5-minute journaling:
Today I am grateful for...

_____

_____

_____

_____

_____

_____

_____

_____

_____

_____

_____

_____

_____

_____

_____

_____

_____

_____

_____

_____

5-minute journaling:
Today I am grateful for...

_____

_____

_____

_____

_____

_____

_____

_____

_____

_____

_____

_____

_____

_____

_____

_____

_____

_____

_____

_____

5-minute journaling:
Today I am grateful for...

_____

_____

_____

_____

_____

_____

_____

_____

_____

_____

_____

_____

_____

_____

_____

_____

_____

5-minute journaling:
Today I am grateful for...

_____

_____

_____

_____

_____

_____

_____

_____

_____

_____

_____

_____

_____

_____

_____

_____

_____

_____

_____

_____

5-minute journaling:
Today I am grateful for...

_____
_____
_____
_____
_____
_____
_____
_____
_____
_____
_____
_____
_____
_____
_____
_____
_____
_____
_____
_____

5-minute journaling:
Today I am grateful for...

_____

_____

_____

_____

_____

_____

_____

_____

_____

_____

_____

_____

_____

_____

_____

_____

_____

_____

_____

Weekly Planner

WEEK OF :

MONTH :

MONDAY

TUESDAY

WEDNESDAY

THURSDAY

FRIDAY

SATURDAY

NOTE :

QUOTE :

ORGANIZING MY THOUGHTS, MANIFESTING MY GOALS 2026

5-minute journaling:
Today I am grateful for...

_____

_____

_____

_____

_____

_____

_____

_____

_____

_____

_____

_____

_____

_____

_____

_____

_____

_____

_____

5-minute journaling:
Today I am grateful for...

_____

_____

_____

_____

_____

_____

_____

_____

_____

_____

_____

_____

_____

_____

_____

_____

_____

_____

5-minute journaling:
Today I am grateful for...

_____

_____

_____

_____

_____

_____

_____

_____

_____

_____

_____

_____

_____

_____

_____

_____

_____

_____

_____

5-minute journaling:
Today I am grateful for...

_____

_____

_____

_____

_____

_____

_____

_____

_____

_____

_____

_____

_____

_____

_____

_____

_____

_____

_____

_____

5-minute journaling:
Today I am grateful for...

_____

_____

_____

_____

_____

_____

_____

_____

_____

_____

_____

_____

_____

_____

_____

_____

_____

_____

_____

_____

_____

5-minute journaling:
Today I am grateful for...

_____

_____

_____

_____

_____

_____

_____

_____

_____

_____

_____

_____

_____

_____

_____

_____

_____

_____

_____

5-minute journaling:
Today I am grateful for...

_____

_____

_____

_____

_____

_____

_____

_____

_____

_____

_____

_____

_____

_____

_____

_____

_____

_____

Weekly Planner

WEEK OF :

MONTH :

MONDAY

TUESDAY

WEDNESDAY

THURSDAY

FRIDAY

SATURDAY

NOTE :

QUOTE :

ORGANIZING MY THOUGHTS, MANIFESTING MY GOALS 2026

5-minute journaling:
Today I am grateful for...

_____
_____
_____
_____
_____
_____
_____
_____
_____
_____
_____
_____
_____
_____
_____
_____
_____
_____
_____
_____
_____

5-minute journaling:
Today I am grateful for...

_____

_____

_____

_____

_____

_____

_____

_____

_____

_____

_____

_____

_____

_____

_____

_____

_____

_____

_____

5-minute journaling:
Today I am grateful for...

_____

_____

_____

_____

_____

_____

_____

_____

_____

_____

_____

_____

_____

_____

_____

_____

_____

_____

5-minute journaling:
Today I am grateful for...

_____

_____

_____

_____

_____

_____

_____

_____

_____

_____

_____

_____

_____

_____

_____

_____

_____

_____

_____

5-minute journaling:
Today I am grateful for...

_____

_____

_____

_____

_____

_____

_____

_____

_____

_____

_____

_____

_____

_____

_____

_____

_____

_____

_____

_____

_____

_____

5-minute journaling:
Today I am grateful for...

_____

_____

_____

_____

_____

_____

_____

_____

_____

_____

_____

_____

_____

_____

_____

_____

_____

_____

_____

_____

5-minute journaling:
Today I am grateful for...

_____

_____

_____

_____

_____

_____

_____

_____

_____

_____

_____

_____

_____

_____

_____

_____

_____

_____

_____

_____

MILESTONE ACCOMPLISHMENT

1) What did I accomplish:

_____

_____

2) When did I accomplish it:

_____

3) How did you accomplish it:

_____

_____

_____

4) What motivated you to accomplish it:

_____

_____

_____

5) Did you face any challenges while accomplishing it:

_____

_____

_____

6) How will you celebrate your accomplishment:

_____

_____

_____

What's On
Your Mind?

★ _____

★ _____

★ _____

Month **MARCH 2026**

Ideas, Tasks, Chores, Wishes, Dreams, Desires

➤ _____

➤ _____

➤ _____

➤ _____

➤ _____

➤ _____

➤ _____

➤ _____

➤ _____

➤ _____

➤ _____

➤ _____

VISION ———— BOARD

Start each month with clarity and purpose. Reflect, plan, manifest. This journal is designed to help you stay organized, set priorities, and achieve your goals.

(Month): _____

Health

Career & Finances

Relationships & Social Life

Travel

Fitness

Spirituality & Mindfulness

Monthly goals

HEALTH GOALS

- ♡ _____
- ♡ _____
- ♡ _____

CAREER AND WORK GOALS

- ♡ _____
- ♡ _____
- ♡ _____

FITNESS GOALS

- ♡ _____
- ♡ _____
- ♡ _____

Monthly goals

RELATIONSHIP & SOCIAL LIFE GOALS

♡ _____

♡ _____

♡ _____

TRAVEL GOALS

♡ _____

♡ _____

♡ _____

SPIRITUAL AND MINDFULNESS GOALS

♡ _____

♡ _____

♡ _____

Monthly goals

FINANCE GOALS

- ♡ _____
- ♡ _____
- ♡ _____

OTHER GOALS

- ♡ _____
- ♡ _____
- ♡ _____

OTHER GOALS

- ♡ _____
- ♡ _____
- ♡ _____

Weekly Planner

WEEK OF :

MONTH :

MONDAY

TUESDAY

WEDNESDAY

THURSDAY

FRIDAY

SATURDAY

NOTE :

QUOTE :

ORGANIZING MY THOUGHTS, MANIFESTING MY GOALS 2026

5-minute journaling:
Today I am grateful for...

_____

_____

_____

_____

_____

_____

_____

_____

_____

_____

_____

_____

_____

_____

_____

_____

_____

_____

_____

5-minute journaling:
Today I am grateful for...

_____
_____
_____
_____
_____
_____
_____
_____
_____
_____
_____
_____
_____
_____
_____
_____
_____
_____
_____
_____

5-minute journaling:
Today I am grateful for...

_____

_____

_____

_____

_____

_____

_____

_____

_____

_____

_____

_____

_____

_____

_____

_____

_____

_____

_____

5-minute journaling:
Today I am grateful for...

_____

_____

_____

_____

_____

_____

_____

_____

_____

_____

_____

_____

_____

_____

_____

_____

_____

_____

_____

5-minute journaling:
Today I am grateful for...

_____

_____

_____

_____

_____

_____

_____

_____

_____

_____

_____

_____

_____

_____

_____

_____

_____

_____

5-minute journaling:
Today I am grateful for...

_____

_____

_____

_____

_____

_____

_____

_____

_____

_____

_____

_____

_____

_____

_____

_____

_____

_____

_____

5-minute journaling:
Today I am grateful for...

_____

_____

_____

_____

_____

_____

_____

_____

_____

_____

_____

_____

_____

_____

_____

_____

_____

_____

_____

_____

_____

_____

_____

Weekly Planner

WEEK OF :

MONTH :

MONDAY

TUESDAY

WEDNESDAY

THURSDAY

FRIDAY

SATURDAY

NOTE :

QUOTE :

ORGANIZING MY THOUGHTS, MANIFESTING MY GOALS 2026

5-minute journaling:
Today I am grateful for...

_____

_____

_____

_____

_____

_____

_____

_____

_____

_____

_____

_____

_____

_____

_____

_____

_____

_____

_____

_____

_____

5-minute journaling:
Today I am grateful for...

_____

_____

_____

_____

_____

_____

_____

_____

_____

_____

_____

_____

_____

_____

_____

_____

_____

_____

_____

5-minute journaling:
Today I am grateful for...

_____
_____
_____
_____
_____
_____
_____
_____
_____
_____
_____
_____
_____
_____
_____
_____
_____
_____
_____
_____
_____

5-minute journaling:
Today I am grateful for...

_____
_____
_____
_____
_____
_____
_____
_____
_____
_____
_____
_____
_____
_____
_____
_____
_____
_____
_____
_____
_____

5-minute journaling:
Today I am grateful for...

_____

_____

_____

_____

_____

_____

_____

_____

_____

_____

_____

_____

_____

_____

_____

_____

_____

_____

_____

_____

_____

_____

_____

_____

5-minute journaling:
Today I am grateful for...

_____

_____

_____

_____

_____

_____

_____

_____

_____

_____

_____

_____

_____

_____

_____

_____

_____

_____

5-minute journaling:
Today I am grateful for...

_____

_____

_____

_____

_____

_____

_____

_____

_____

_____

_____

_____

_____

_____

_____

_____

_____

_____

_____

_____

_____

Weekly Planner

WEEK OF :

MONTH :

MONDAY

TUESDAY

WEDNESDAY

THURSDAY

FRIDAY

SATURDAY

NOTE :

QUOTE :

ORGANIZING MY THOUGHTS, MANIFESTING MY GOALS 2026

5-minute journaling:
Today I am grateful for...

_____

_____

_____

_____

_____

_____

_____

_____

_____

_____

_____

_____

_____

_____

_____

_____

_____

_____

5-minute journaling:
Today I am grateful for...

_____

_____

_____

_____

_____

_____

_____

_____

_____

_____

_____

_____

_____

_____

_____

_____

_____

_____

_____

_____

5-minute journaling:
Today I am grateful for...

_____

_____

_____

_____

_____

_____

_____

_____

_____

_____

_____

_____

_____

_____

_____

_____

_____

_____

_____

_____

_____

5-minute journaling:
Today I am grateful for...

_____
_____
_____
_____
_____
_____
_____
_____
_____
_____
_____
_____
_____
_____
_____
_____
_____
_____
_____

5-minute journaling:
Today I am grateful for...

_____

_____

_____

_____

_____

_____

_____

_____

_____

_____

_____

_____

_____

_____

_____

_____

_____

_____

_____

_____

_____

5-minute journaling:
Today I am grateful for...

_____
_____
_____
_____
_____
_____
_____
_____
_____
_____
_____
_____
_____
_____
_____
_____
_____
_____
_____
_____
_____

5-minute journaling:
Today I am grateful for...

_____

_____

_____

_____

_____

_____

_____

_____

_____

_____

_____

_____

_____

_____

_____

_____

_____

_____

_____

Weekly Planner

WEEK OF :

MONTH :

MONDAY

TUESDAY

WEDNESDAY

THURSDAY

FRIDAY

SATURDAY

NOTE :

QUOTE :

ORGANIZING MY THOUGHTS, MANIFESTING MY GOALS 2026

5-minute journaling:
Today I am grateful for...

_____

_____

_____

_____

_____

_____

_____

_____

_____

_____

_____

_____

_____

_____

_____

_____

_____

_____

_____

_____

_____

5-minute journaling:
Today I am grateful for...

_____
_____
_____
_____
_____
_____
_____
_____
_____
_____
_____
_____
_____
_____
_____
_____
_____
_____
_____

5-minute journaling:
Today I am grateful for...

_____

_____

_____

_____

_____

_____

_____

_____

_____

_____

_____

_____

_____

_____

_____

_____

_____

_____

_____

_____

_____

5-minute journaling:
Today I am grateful for...

_____

_____

_____

_____

_____

_____

_____

_____

_____

_____

_____

_____

_____

_____

_____

_____

_____

_____

_____

5-minute journaling:
Today I am grateful for...

_____

_____

_____

_____

_____

_____

_____

_____

_____

_____

_____

_____

_____

_____

_____

_____

_____

_____

_____

_____

5-minute journaling:
Today I am grateful for...

_____
_____
_____
_____
_____
_____
_____
_____
_____
_____
_____
_____
_____
_____
_____
_____
_____
_____
_____

5-minute journaling:
Today I am grateful for...

_____

_____

_____

_____

_____

_____

_____

_____

_____

_____

_____

_____

_____

_____

_____

_____

_____

_____

_____

_____

Weekly Planner

WEEK OF :

MONTH :

MONDAY

TUESDAY

WEDNESDAY

THURSDAY

FRIDAY

SATURDAY

NOTE :

QUOTE :

ORGANIZING MY THOUGHTS, MANIFESTING MY GOALS 2026

5-minute journaling:
Today I am grateful for...

_____

_____

_____

_____

_____

_____

_____

_____

_____

_____

_____

_____

_____

_____

_____

_____

_____

_____

_____

_____

_____

5-minute journaling:
Today I am grateful for...

_____

_____

_____

_____

_____

_____

_____

_____

_____

_____

_____

_____

_____

_____

_____

_____

_____

_____

_____

_____

_____

_____

5-minute journaling:
Today I am grateful for...

_____
_____
_____
_____
_____
_____
_____
_____
_____
_____
_____
_____
_____
_____
_____
_____
_____
_____
_____
_____

MILESTONE ACCOMPLISHMENT

1) What did I accomplish:

_____

_____

2) When did I accomplish it:

_____

3) How did you accomplish it:

_____

_____

_____

4) What motivated you to accomplish it:

_____

_____

_____

5) Did you face any challenges while accomplishing it:

_____

_____

_____

6) How will you celebrate your accomplishment:

_____

_____

_____

What's On Your Mind?

★ _____

★ _____

★ _____

Month **APRIL 2026**

Ideas, Tasks, Chores, Wishes, Dreams, Desires

➤ _____

➤ _____

➤ _____

➤ _____

➤ _____

➤ _____

➤ _____

➤ _____

➤ _____

➤ _____

➤ _____

➤ _____

➤ _____

➤ _____

VISION —————— BOARD

Start each month with clarity and purpose. Reflect, plan, manifest. This journal is designed to help you stay organized, set priorities, and achieve your goals.

(Month): _____

Health

Career & Finances

Relationships & Social Life

Travel

Fitness

Spirituality & Mindfulness

Monthly goals

HEALTH GOALS

- ♡ _____
- ♡ _____
- ♡ _____

CAREER AND WORK GOALS

- ♡ _____
- ♡ _____
- ♡ _____

FITNESS GOALS

- ♡ _____
- ♡ _____
- ♡ _____

Monthly goals

RELATIONSHIP & SOCIAL LIFE GOALS

♡ _____

♡ _____

♡ _____

TRAVEL GOALS

♡ _____

♡ _____

♡ _____

SPIRITUAL AND MINDFULNESS GOALS

♡ _____

♡ _____

♡ _____

Monthly goals

FINANCE GOALS

- ♡ _____
- ♡ _____
- ♡ _____

OTHER GOALS

- ♡ _____
- ♡ _____
- ♡ _____

OTHER GOALS

- ♡ _____
- ♡ _____
- ♡ _____

Weekly Planner

WEEK OF :

MONTH :

MONDAY

TUESDAY

WEDNESDAY

THURSDAY

FRIDAY

SATURDAY

NOTE :

QUOTE :

ORGANIZING MY THOUGHTS, MANIFESTING MY GOALS 2026

5-minute journaling:
Today I am grateful for...

_____

_____

_____

_____

_____

_____

_____

_____

_____

_____

_____

_____

_____

_____

_____

_____

_____

_____

_____

_____

5-minute journaling:
Today I am grateful for...

_____

_____

_____

_____

_____

_____

_____

_____

_____

_____

_____

_____

_____

_____

_____

_____

_____

_____

_____

5-minute journaling:
Today I am grateful for...

_____

_____

_____

_____

_____

_____

_____

_____

_____

_____

_____

_____

_____

_____

_____

_____

_____

_____

5-minute journaling:
Today I am grateful for...

_____

_____

_____

_____

_____

_____

_____

_____

_____

_____

_____

_____

_____

_____

_____

_____

_____

_____

_____

_____

Weekly Planner

WEEK OF :

MONTH :

MONDAY

TUESDAY

WEDNESDAY

THURSDAY

FRIDAY

SATURDAY

NOTE :

QUOTE :

ORGANIZING MY THOUGHTS, MANIFESTING MY GOALS 2026

5-minute journaling:
Today I am grateful for...

_____
_____
_____
_____
_____
_____
_____
_____
_____
_____
_____
_____
_____
_____
_____
_____
_____
_____
_____

5-minute journaling:
Today I am grateful for...

_____

_____

_____

_____

_____

_____

_____

_____

_____

_____

_____

_____

_____

_____

_____

_____

_____

_____

_____

_____

_____

5-minute journaling:
Today I am grateful for...

_____

_____

_____

_____

_____

_____

_____

_____

_____

_____

_____

_____

_____

_____

_____

_____

_____

_____

_____

5-minute journaling:
Today I am grateful for...

_____

_____

_____

_____

_____

_____

_____

_____

_____

_____

_____

_____

_____

_____

_____

_____

_____

_____

_____

5-minute journaling:
Today I am grateful for...

_____
_____
_____
_____
_____
_____
_____
_____
_____
_____
_____
_____
_____
_____
_____
_____
_____
_____
_____

5-minute journaling:
Today I am grateful for...

_____

_____

_____

_____

_____

_____

_____

_____

_____

_____

_____

_____

_____

_____

_____

_____

_____

_____

_____

_____

5-minute journaling:
Today I am grateful for...

_____

_____

_____

_____

_____

_____

_____

_____

_____

_____

_____

_____

_____

_____

_____

_____

_____

_____

_____

Weekly Planner

WEEK OF :

MONTH :

MONDAY

TUESDAY

WEDNESDAY

THURSDAY

FRIDAY

SATURDAY

NOTE :

QUOTE :

ORGANIZING MY THOUGHTS, MANIFESTING MY GOALS 2026

5-minute journaling:
Today I am grateful for...

_____
_____
_____
_____
_____
_____
_____
_____
_____
_____
_____
_____
_____
_____
_____
_____
_____
_____
_____
_____

5-minute journaling:
Today I am grateful for...

_____
_____
_____
_____
_____
_____
_____
_____
_____
_____
_____
_____
_____
_____
_____
_____
_____
_____
_____
_____
_____

5-minute journaling:
Today I am grateful for...

_____

_____

_____

_____

_____

_____

_____

_____

_____

_____

_____

_____

_____

_____

_____

_____

_____

_____

_____

5-minute journaling:
Today I am grateful for...

_____

_____

_____

_____

_____

_____

_____

_____

_____

_____

_____

_____

_____

_____

_____

_____

_____

_____

_____

_____

_____

5-minute journaling:
Today I am grateful for...

_____
_____
_____
_____
_____
_____
_____
_____
_____
_____
_____
_____
_____
_____
_____
_____
_____
_____
_____

5-minute journaling:
Today I am grateful for...

_____

_____

_____

_____

_____

_____

_____

_____

_____

_____

_____

_____

_____

_____

_____

_____

_____

_____

_____

_____

5-minute journaling:
Today I am grateful for...

_____

_____

_____

_____

_____

_____

_____

_____

_____

_____

_____

_____

_____

_____

_____

_____

_____

_____

_____

_____

Weekly Planner

MONDAY

TUESDAY

WEDNESDAY

THURSDAY

FRIDAY

SATURDAY

NOTE :

QUOTE :

ORGANIZING MY THOUGHTS, MANIFESTING MY GOALS 2026

5-minute journaling:
Today I am grateful for...

_____

_____

_____

_____

_____

_____

_____

_____

_____

_____

_____

_____

_____

_____

_____

_____

_____

_____

_____

5-minute journaling:
Today I am grateful for...

_____

_____

_____

_____

_____

_____

_____

_____

_____

_____

_____

_____

_____

_____

_____

_____

_____

_____

_____

_____

5-minute journaling:
Today I am grateful for...

_____

_____

_____

_____

_____

_____

_____

_____

_____

_____

_____

_____

_____

_____

_____

_____

_____

_____

_____

5-minute journaling:
Today I am grateful for...

_____

_____

_____

_____

_____

_____

_____

_____

_____

_____

_____

_____

_____

_____

_____

_____

_____

_____

_____

_____

5-minute journaling:
Today I am grateful for...

_____

_____

_____

_____

_____

_____

_____

_____

_____

_____

_____

_____

_____

_____

_____

_____

_____

_____

_____

5-minute journaling:
Today I am grateful for...

_____

_____

_____

_____

_____

_____

_____

_____

_____

_____

_____

_____

_____

_____

_____

_____

_____

_____

_____

_____

5-minute journaling:
Today I am grateful for...

_____

_____

_____

_____

_____

_____

_____

_____

_____

_____

_____

_____

_____

_____

_____

_____

_____

_____

_____

_____

Weekly Planner

WEEK OF :

MONTH :

MONDAY	TUESDAY	WEDNESDAY

THURSDAY	FRIDAY	SATURDAY

NOTE :

QUOTE :

ORGANIZING MY THOUGHTS, MANIFESTING MY GOALS 2026

5-minute journaling:
Today I am grateful for...

_____
_____
_____
_____
_____
_____
_____
_____
_____
_____
_____
_____
_____
_____
_____
_____
_____
_____
_____

5-minute journaling:
Today I am grateful for...

_____
_____
_____
_____
_____
_____
_____
_____
_____
_____
_____
_____
_____
_____
_____
_____
_____
_____
_____
_____
_____

5-minute journaling:
Today I am grateful for...

_____

_____

_____

_____

_____

_____

_____

_____

_____

_____

_____

_____

_____

_____

_____

_____

_____

_____

_____

5-minute journaling:
Today I am grateful for...

_____

_____

_____

_____

_____

_____

_____

_____

_____

_____

_____

_____

_____

_____

_____

_____

_____

_____

_____

_____

5-minute journaling:
Today I am grateful for...

_____

_____

_____

_____

_____

_____

_____

_____

_____

_____

_____

_____

_____

_____

_____

_____

_____

_____

MILESTONE ACCOMPLISHMENT

1) What did I accomplish:

_____

_____

2) When did I accomplish it:

_____

3) How did you accomplish it:

_____

_____

_____

4) What motivated you to accomplish it:

_____

_____

_____

5) Did you face any challenges while accomplishing it:

_____

_____

_____

6) How will you celebrate your accomplishment:

_____

_____

_____

What's On Your Mind?

★ _____

★ _____

★ _____

Month **MAY 2026**

Ideas, Tasks, Chores, Wishes, Dreams, Desires

➤ _____

➤ _____

➤ _____

➤ _____

➤ _____

➤ _____

➤ _____

➤ _____

➤ _____

➤ _____

➤ _____

➤ _____

➤ _____

VISION ———————— BOARD

Start each month with clarity and purpose. Reflect, plan, manifest. This journal is designed to help you stay organized, set priorities, and achieve your goals.

(Month): _____

Health

Career & Finances

Relationships & Social Life

Travel

Fitness

Spirituality & Mindfulness

Monthly goals

HEALTH GOALS

- ♡ _____
- ♡ _____
- ♡ _____

CAREER AND WORK GOALS

- ♡ _____
- ♡ _____
- ♡ _____

FITNESS GOALS

- ♡ _____
- ♡ _____
- ♡ _____

Monthly goals

RELATIONSHIP & SOCIAL LIFE GOALS

♡ _____

♡ _____

♡ _____

TRAVEL GOALS

♡ _____

♡ _____

♡ _____

SPIRITUAL AND MINDFULNESS GOALS

♡ _____

♡ _____

♡ _____

Monthly goals

FINANCE GOALS

- ♡ _____
- ♡ _____
- ♡ _____

OTHER GOALS

- ♡ _____
- ♡ _____
- ♡ _____

OTHER GOALS

- ♡ _____
- ♡ _____
- ♡ _____

Weekly Planner

WEEK OF :

MONTH :

MONDAY

TUESDAY

WEDNESDAY

THURSDAY

FRIDAY

SATURDAY

NOTE :

QUOTE :

ORGANIZING MY THOUGHTS, MANIFESTING MY GOALS 2026

5-minute journaling:
Today I am grateful for...

_____

_____

_____

_____

_____

_____

_____

_____

_____

_____

_____

_____

_____

_____

_____

_____

_____

5-minute journaling:
Today I am grateful for...

_____

_____

_____

_____

_____

_____

_____

_____

_____

_____

_____

_____

_____

_____

_____

_____

_____

_____

Weekly Planner

WEEK OF :

MONTH :

MONDAY

TUESDAY

WEDNESDAY

THURSDAY

FRIDAY

SATURDAY

NOTE :

QUOTE :

ORGANIZING MY THOUGHTS, MANIFESTING MY GOALS 2026

5-minute journaling:
Today I am grateful for...

_____

_____

_____

_____

_____

_____

_____

_____

_____

_____

_____

_____

_____

_____

_____

_____

_____

_____

_____

_____

_____

5-minute journaling:
Today I am grateful for...

_____

_____

_____

_____

_____

_____

_____

_____

_____

_____

_____

_____

_____

_____

_____

_____

_____

5-minute journaling:
Today I am grateful for...

_____

_____

_____

_____

_____

_____

_____

_____

_____

_____

_____

_____

_____

_____

_____

_____

_____

_____

5-minute journaling:
Today I am grateful for...

_____

_____

_____

_____

_____

_____

_____

_____

_____

_____

_____

_____

_____

_____

_____

_____

_____

_____

5-minute journaling:
Today I am grateful for...

_____

_____

_____

_____

_____

_____

_____

_____

_____

_____

_____

_____

_____

_____

_____

_____

_____

_____

_____

_____

_____

5-minute journaling:
Today I am grateful for...

_____

_____

_____

_____

_____

_____

_____

_____

_____

_____

_____

_____

_____

_____

_____

_____

_____

_____

_____

5-minute journaling:
Today I am grateful for...

_____
_____
_____
_____
_____
_____
_____
_____
_____
_____
_____
_____
_____
_____
_____
_____
_____
_____

Weekly Planner

WEEK OF :

MONTH :

MONDAY

TUESDAY

WEDNESDAY

THURSDAY

FRIDAY

SATURDAY

NOTE :

QUOTE :

ORGANIZING MY THOUGHTS, MANIFESTING MY GOALS 2026

5-minute journaling:
Today I am grateful for...

_____

_____

_____

_____

_____

_____

_____

_____

_____

_____

_____

_____

_____

_____

_____

_____

_____

_____

_____

_____

5-minute journaling:
Today I am grateful for...

_____

_____

_____

_____

_____

_____

_____

_____

_____

_____

_____

_____

_____

_____

_____

_____

_____

_____

_____

5-minute journaling:
Today I am grateful for...

_____

_____

_____

_____

_____

_____

_____

_____

_____

_____

_____

_____

_____

_____

_____

_____

_____

_____

_____

_____

_____

_____

5-minute journaling:
Today I am grateful for...

_____

_____

_____

_____

_____

_____

_____

_____

_____

_____

_____

_____

_____

_____

_____

_____

_____

_____

_____

_____

5-minute journaling:
Today I am grateful for...

_____

_____

_____

_____

_____

_____

_____

_____

_____

_____

_____

_____

_____

_____

_____

_____

_____

_____

5-minute journaling:
Today I am grateful for...

_____
_____
_____
_____
_____
_____
_____
_____
_____
_____
_____
_____
_____
_____
_____
_____
_____
_____
_____
_____
_____

5-minute journaling:
Today I am grateful for...

_____

_____

_____

_____

_____

_____

_____

_____

_____

_____

_____

_____

_____

_____

_____

_____

_____

_____

_____

Weekly Planner

WEEK OF :

MONTH :

MONDAY

TUESDAY

WEDNESDAY

THURSDAY

FRIDAY

SATURDAY

NOTE :

QUOTE :

ORGANIZING MY THOUGHTS, MANIFESTING MY GOALS 2026

5-minute journaling:
Today I am grateful for...

_____

_____

_____

_____

_____

_____

_____

_____

_____

_____

_____

_____

_____

_____

_____

_____

_____

_____

_____

_____

_____

5-minute journaling:
Today I am grateful for...

_____

_____

_____

_____

_____

_____

_____

_____

_____

_____

_____

_____

_____

_____

_____

_____

_____

_____

_____

_____

_____

5-minute journaling:
Today I am grateful for...

_____

_____

_____

_____

_____

_____

_____

_____

_____

_____

_____

_____

_____

_____

_____

_____

_____

_____

_____

_____

_____

5-minute journaling:
Today I am grateful for...

_____

_____

_____

_____

_____

_____

_____

_____

_____

_____

_____

_____

_____

_____

_____

_____

_____

_____

_____

5-minute journaling:
Today I am grateful for...

_____

_____

_____

_____

_____

_____

_____

_____

_____

_____

_____

_____

_____

_____

_____

_____

_____

_____

_____

_____

5-minute journaling:
Today I am grateful for...

_____

_____

_____

_____

_____

_____

_____

_____

_____

_____

_____

_____

_____

_____

_____

_____

_____

_____

_____

5-minute journaling:
Today I am grateful for...

_____

_____

_____

_____

_____

_____

_____

_____

_____

_____

_____

_____

_____

_____

_____

_____

_____

_____

_____

_____

Weekly Planner

WEEK OF :

MONTH :

MONDAY

TUESDAY

WEDNESDAY

THURSDAY

FRIDAY

SATURDAY

NOTE :

QUOTE :

ORGANIZING MY THOUGHTS, MANIFESTING MY GOALS 2026

5-minute journaling:
Today I am grateful for...

_____

_____

_____

_____

_____

_____

_____

_____

_____

_____

_____

_____

_____

_____

_____

_____

_____

_____

_____

_____

_____

5-minute journaling:
Today I am grateful for...

_____

_____

_____

_____

_____

_____

_____

_____

_____

_____

_____

_____

_____

_____

_____

_____

_____

_____

_____

5-minute journaling:
Today I am grateful for...

_____

_____

_____

_____

_____

_____

_____

_____

_____

_____

_____

_____

_____

_____

_____

_____

_____

_____

_____

_____

_____

5-minute journaling:
Today I am grateful for...

_____

_____

_____

_____

_____

_____

_____

_____

_____

_____

_____

_____

_____

_____

_____

_____

_____

_____

_____

5-minute journaling:
Today I am grateful for...

_____
_____
_____
_____
_____
_____
_____
_____
_____
_____
_____
_____
_____
_____
_____
_____
_____
_____
_____

5-minute journaling:
Today I am grateful for...

_____

_____

_____

_____

_____

_____

_____

_____

_____

_____

_____

_____

_____

_____

_____

_____

_____

_____

_____

5-minute journaling:
Today I am grateful for...

_____

_____

_____

_____

_____

_____

_____

_____

_____

_____

_____

_____

_____

_____

_____

_____

_____

_____

_____

_____

_____

Weekly Planner

WEEK OF :

MONTH :

MONDAY

TUESDAY

WEDNESDAY

THURSDAY

FRIDAY

SATURDAY

NOTE :

QUOTE :

ORGANIZING MY THOUGHTS, MANIFESTING MY GOALS 2026

5-minute journaling:
Today I am grateful for...

_____

_____

_____

_____

_____

_____

_____

_____

_____

_____

_____

_____

_____

_____

_____

_____

_____

_____

_____

_____

_____

MILESTONE ACCOMPLISHMENT

1) What did I accomplish:

_____

_____

2) When did I accomplish it: _____

3) How did you accomplish it:

_____

_____

_____

4) What motivated you to accomplish it:

_____

_____

_____

5) Did you face any challenges while accomplishing it:

_____

_____

_____

6) How will you celebrate your accomplishment:

_____

_____

_____

What's On Your Mind?

★ _____

★ _____

★ _____

Month **JUNE 2026**

Ideas, Tasks, Chores, Wishes, Dreams, Desires

➤ _____

➤ _____

➤ _____

➤ _____

➤ _____

➤ _____

➤ _____

➤ _____

➤ _____

➤ _____

➤ _____

➤ _____

➤ _____

➤ _____

VISION ——————— BOARD

Start each month with clarity and purpose. Reflect, plan, manifest. This journal is designed to help you stay organized, set priorities, and achieve your goals.

(Month): _____

Health

Career & Finances

Relationships & Social Life

Travel

Fitness

Spirituality & Mindfulness

Monthly goals

HEALTH GOALS

- ♡ _____
- ♡ _____
- ♡ _____

CAREER AND WORK GOALS

- ♡ _____
- ♡ _____
- ♡ _____

FITNESS GOALS

- ♡ _____
- ♡ _____
- ♡ _____

Monthly goals

RELATIONSHIP & SOCIAL LIFE GOALS

♡ _____

♡ _____

♡ _____

TRAVEL GOALS

♡ _____

♡ _____

♡ _____

SPIRITUAL AND MINDFULNESS GOALS

♡ _____

♡ _____

♡ _____

Monthly goals

FINANCE GOALS

♡ _____
♡ _____
♡ _____

OTHER GOALS

♡ _____
♡ _____
♡ _____

OTHER GOALS

♡ _____
♡ _____
♡ _____

Weekly Planner

WEEK OF :

MONTH :

MONDAY

TUESDAY

WEDNESDAY

THURSDAY

FRIDAY

SATURDAY

NOTE :

QUOTE :

ORGANIZING MY THOUGHTS, MANIFESTING MY GOALS 2026

5-minute journaling:
Today I am grateful for...

_____

_____

_____

_____

_____

_____

_____

_____

_____

_____

_____

_____

_____

_____

_____

_____

_____

_____

_____

_____

5-minute journaling:
Today I am grateful for...

_____
_____
_____
_____
_____
_____
_____
_____
_____
_____
_____
_____
_____
_____
_____
_____
_____
_____
_____
_____

5-minute journaling:
Today I am grateful for...

_____

_____

_____

_____

_____

_____

_____

_____

_____

_____

_____

_____

_____

_____

_____

_____

_____

_____

_____

5-minute journaling:
Today I am grateful for...

_____

_____

_____

_____

_____

_____

_____

_____

_____

_____

_____

_____

_____

_____

_____

_____

_____

_____

5-minute journaling:
Today I am grateful for...

_____

_____

_____

_____

_____

_____

_____

_____

_____

_____

_____

_____

_____

_____

_____

_____

_____

_____

5-minute journaling:
Today I am grateful for...

_____

_____

_____

_____

_____

_____

_____

_____

_____

_____

_____

_____

_____

_____

_____

_____

_____

_____

_____

_____

Weekly Planner

WEEK OF :

MONTH :

MONDAY

TUESDAY

WEDNESDAY

THURSDAY

FRIDAY

SATURDAY

NOTE :

QUOTE :

ORGANIZING MY THOUGHTS, MANIFESTING MY GOALS 2026

5-minute journaling:
Today I am grateful for...

_____

_____

_____

_____

_____

_____

_____

_____

_____

_____

_____

_____

_____

_____

_____

_____

_____

_____

_____

5-minute journaling:
Today I am grateful for...

_____

_____

_____

_____

_____

_____

_____

_____

_____

_____

_____

_____

_____

_____

_____

_____

_____

_____

_____

_____

_____

5-minute journaling:
Today I am grateful for...

_____

_____

_____

_____

_____

_____

_____

_____

_____

_____

_____

_____

_____

_____

_____

_____

_____

_____

_____

_____

5-minute journaling:
Today I am grateful for...

_____
_____
_____
_____
_____
_____
_____
_____
_____
_____
_____
_____
_____
_____
_____
_____
_____
_____
_____
_____

5-minute journaling:
Today I am grateful for...

_____
_____
_____
_____
_____
_____
_____
_____
_____
_____
_____
_____
_____
_____
_____
_____
_____
_____
_____
_____

5-minute journaling:
Today I am grateful for...

_____

_____

_____

_____

_____

_____

_____

_____

_____

_____

_____

_____

_____

_____

_____

_____

_____

_____

_____

_____

5-minute journaling:
Today I am grateful for...

_____
_____
_____
_____
_____
_____
_____
_____
_____
_____
_____
_____
_____
_____
_____
_____
_____
_____
_____

Weekly Planner

WEEK OF :

MONTH :

MONDAY

TUESDAY

WEDNESDAY

THURSDAY

FRIDAY

SATURDAY

NOTE :

QUOTE :

ORGANIZING MY THOUGHTS, MANIFESTING MY GOALS 2026

5-minute journaling:
Today I am grateful for...

_____

_____

_____

_____

_____

_____

_____

_____

_____

_____

_____

_____

_____

_____

_____

_____

_____

_____

_____

5-minute journaling:
Today I am grateful for...

_____

_____

_____

_____

_____

_____

_____

_____

_____

_____

_____

_____

_____

_____

_____

_____

_____

_____

_____

_____

5-minute journaling:
Today I am grateful for...

_____

_____

_____

_____

_____

_____

_____

_____

_____

_____

_____

_____

_____

_____

_____

_____

_____

_____

5-minute journaling:
Today I am grateful for...

_____

_____

_____

_____

_____

_____

_____

_____

_____

_____

_____

_____

_____

_____

_____

_____

_____

_____

5-minute journaling:
Today I am grateful for...

_____

_____

_____

_____

_____

_____

_____

_____

_____

_____

_____

_____

_____

_____

_____

_____

_____

_____

_____

5-minute journaling:
Today I am grateful for...

_____

_____

_____

_____

_____

_____

_____

_____

_____

_____

_____

_____

_____

_____

_____

_____

_____

_____

_____

_____

5-minute journaling:
Today I am grateful for...

_____

_____

_____

_____

_____

_____

_____

_____

_____

_____

_____

_____

_____

_____

_____

_____

_____

_____

_____

Weekly Planner

WEEK OF :

MONTH :

MONDAY

TUESDAY

WEDNESDAY

THURSDAY

FRIDAY

SATURDAY

NOTE :

QUOTE :

ORGANIZING MY THOUGHTS, MANIFESTING MY GOALS 2026

5-minute journaling:
Today I am grateful for...

_____

_____

_____

_____

_____

_____

_____

_____

_____

_____

_____

_____

_____

_____

_____

_____

_____

_____

_____

5-minute journaling:
Today I am grateful for...

_____

_____

_____

_____

_____

_____

_____

_____

_____

_____

_____

_____

_____

_____

_____

_____

_____

_____

_____

_____

_____

5-minute journaling:
Today I am grateful for...

_____

_____

_____

_____

_____

_____

_____

_____

_____

_____

_____

_____

_____

_____

_____

_____

_____

_____

_____

_____

5-minute journaling:
Today I am grateful for...

_____

_____

_____

_____

_____

_____

_____

_____

_____

_____

_____

_____

_____

_____

_____

_____

_____

_____

5-minute journaling:
Today I am grateful for...

_____
_____
_____
_____
_____
_____
_____
_____
_____
_____
_____
_____
_____
_____
_____
_____
_____
_____
_____

5-minute journaling:
Today I am grateful for...

_____

_____

_____

_____

_____

_____

_____

_____

_____

_____

_____

_____

_____

_____

_____

_____

_____

_____

_____

_____

_____

5-minute journaling:
Today I am grateful for...

_____

_____

_____

_____

_____

_____

_____

_____

_____

_____

_____

_____

_____

_____

_____

_____

_____

_____

_____

Weekly Planner

WEEK OF :

MONTH :

MONDAY

TUESDAY

WEDNESDAY

THURSDAY

FRIDAY

SATURDAY

NOTE :

QUOTE :

ORGANIZING MY THOUGHTS, MANIFESTING MY GOALS 2026

5-minute journaling:
Today I am grateful for...

_____

_____

_____

_____

_____

_____

_____

_____

_____

_____

_____

_____

_____

_____

_____

_____

_____

_____

_____

5-minute journaling:
Today I am grateful for...

_____
_____
_____
_____
_____
_____
_____
_____
_____
_____
_____
_____
_____
_____
_____
_____
_____
_____
_____
_____
_____

5-minute journaling:
Today I am grateful for...

_____

_____

_____

_____

_____

_____

_____

_____

_____

_____

_____

_____

_____

_____

_____

_____

_____

_____

_____

_____

MILESTONE ACCOMPLISHMENT

1) What did I accomplish:

_____

_____

2) When did I accomplish it:

_____

3) How did you accomplish it:

_____

_____

_____

4) What motivated you to accomplish it:

_____

_____

_____

5) Did you face any challenges while accomplishing it:

_____

_____

_____

6) How will you celebrate your accomplishment:

_____

_____

_____

What's On
Your Mind?

★ _____

★ _____

★ _____

Month   **JULY 2026**

Ideas, Tasks, Chores, Wishes, Dreams, Desires

➤ _____

➤ _____

➤ _____

➤ _____

➤ _____

➤ _____

➤ _____

➤ _____

➤ _____

➤ _____

➤ _____

➤ _____

VISION ——————— BOARD

Start each month with clarity and purpose. Reflect, plan, manifest. This journal is designed to help you stay organized, set priorities, and achieve your goals.

(Month): _____

Health

Career & Finances

Relationships & Social Life

Travel

Fitness

Spirituality & Mindfulness

Monthly goals

HEALTH GOALS

- ♡ _____
- ♡ _____
- ♡ _____

CAREER AND WORK GOALS

- ♡ _____
- ♡ _____
- ♡ _____

FITNESS GOALS

- ♡ _____
- ♡ _____
- ♡ _____

Monthly goals

RELATIONSHIP & SOCIAL LIFE GOALS

♡ _____

♡ _____

♡ _____

TRAVEL GOALS

♡ _____

♡ _____

♡ _____

SPIRITUAL AND MINDFULNESS GOALS

♡ _____

♡ _____

♡ _____

Monthly goals

FINANCE GOALS

- ♡ _____
- ♡ _____
- ♡ _____

OTHER GOALS

- ♡ _____
- ♡ _____
- ♡ _____

OTHER GOALS

- ♡ _____
- ♡ _____
- ♡ _____

Weekly Planner

WEEK OF :

MONTH :

MONDAY

TUESDAY

WEDNESDAY

THURSDAY

FRIDAY

SATURDAY

NOTE :

QUOTE :

ORGANIZING MY THOUGHTS, MANIFESTING MY GOALS 2026

5-minute journaling:
Today I am grateful for...

_____

_____

_____

_____

_____

_____

_____

_____

_____

_____

_____

_____

_____

_____

_____

_____

_____

_____

5-minute journaling:
Today I am grateful for...

_____

_____

_____

_____

_____

_____

_____

_____

_____

_____

_____

_____

_____

_____

_____

_____

_____

_____

_____

_____

5-minute journaling:
Today I am grateful for...

_____
_____
_____
_____
_____
_____
_____
_____
_____
_____
_____
_____
_____
_____
_____
_____
_____
_____
_____
_____
_____

5-minute journaling:
Today I am grateful for...

_____
_____
_____
_____
_____
_____
_____
_____
_____
_____
_____
_____
_____
_____
_____
_____
_____
_____
_____

Weekly Planner

WEEK OF :

MONTH :

MONDAY

TUESDAY

WEDNESDAY

THURSDAY

FRIDAY

SATURDAY

NOTE :

QUOTE :

ORGANIZING MY THOUGHTS, MANIFESTING MY GOALS 2026

5-minute journaling:
Today I am grateful for...

_____

_____

_____

_____

_____

_____

_____

_____

_____

_____

_____

_____

_____

_____

_____

_____

_____

_____

_____

5-minute journaling:
Today I am grateful for...

_____

_____

_____

_____

_____

_____

_____

_____

_____

_____

_____

_____

_____

_____

_____

_____

_____

_____

_____

_____

_____

_____

5-minute journaling:
Today I am grateful for...

_____

_____

_____

_____

_____

_____

_____

_____

_____

_____

_____

_____

_____

_____

_____

_____

_____

_____

_____

_____

_____

5-minute journaling:
Today I am grateful for...

_____

_____

_____

_____

_____

_____

_____

_____

_____

_____

_____

_____

_____

_____

_____

_____

_____

_____

_____

_____

_____

5-minute journaling:
Today I am grateful for...

_____

_____

_____

_____

_____

_____

_____

_____

_____

_____

_____

_____

_____

_____

_____

_____

_____

_____

_____

_____

5-minute journaling:
Today I am grateful for...

_____

_____

_____

_____

_____

_____

_____

_____

_____

_____

_____

_____

_____

_____

_____

_____

_____

_____

5-minute journaling:
Today I am grateful for...

_____
_____
_____
_____
_____
_____
_____
_____
_____
_____
_____
_____
_____
_____
_____
_____
_____
_____
_____

Weekly Planner

WEEK OF :

MONTH :

MONDAY

TUESDAY

WEDNESDAY

THURSDAY

FRIDAY

SATURDAY

NOTE :

QUOTE :

ORGANIZING MY THOUGHTS, MANIFESTING MY GOALS 2026

5-minute journaling:
Today I am grateful for...

_____

_____

_____

_____

_____

_____

_____

_____

_____

_____

_____

_____

_____

_____

_____

_____

_____

_____

_____

_____

_____

5-minute journaling:
Today I am grateful for...

_____

_____

_____

_____

_____

_____

_____

_____

_____

_____

_____

_____

_____

_____

_____

_____

_____

_____

_____

5-minute journaling:
Today I am grateful for...

_____

_____

_____

_____

_____

_____

_____

_____

_____

_____

_____

_____

_____

_____

_____

_____

_____

_____

_____

_____

_____

5-minute journaling:
Today I am grateful for...

_____

_____

_____

_____

_____

_____

_____

_____

_____

_____

_____

_____

_____

_____

_____

_____

_____

_____

_____

5-minute journaling:
Today I am grateful for...

_____

_____

_____

_____

_____

_____

_____

_____

_____

_____

_____

_____

_____

_____

_____

_____

_____

_____

_____

_____

5-minute journaling:
Today I am grateful for...

_____
_____
_____
_____
_____
_____
_____
_____
_____
_____
_____
_____
_____
_____
_____
_____
_____
_____
_____

5-minute journaling:
Today I am grateful for...

_____

_____

_____

_____

_____

_____

_____

_____

_____

_____

_____

_____

_____

_____

_____

_____

_____

_____

_____

_____

Weekly Planner

WEEK OF :

MONTH :

MONDAY

TUESDAY

WEDNESDAY

THURSDAY

FRIDAY

SATURDAY

NOTE :

QUOTE :

ORGANIZING MY THOUGHTS, MANIFESTING MY GOALS 2026

5-minute journaling:
Today I am grateful for...

_____

_____

_____

_____

_____

_____

_____

_____

_____

_____

_____

_____

_____

_____

_____

_____

_____

_____

_____

_____

5-minute journaling:
Today I am grateful for...

_____

_____

_____

_____

_____

_____

_____

_____

_____

_____

_____

_____

_____

_____

_____

_____

_____

_____

_____

_____

_____

5-minute journaling:
Today I am grateful for...

_____
_____
_____
_____
_____
_____
_____
_____
_____
_____
_____
_____
_____
_____
_____
_____
_____
_____
_____
_____

5-minute journaling:
Today I am grateful for...

_____

_____

_____

_____

_____

_____

_____

_____

_____

_____

_____

_____

_____

_____

_____

_____

_____

_____

_____

5-minute journaling:
Today I am grateful for...

_____

_____

_____

_____

_____

_____

_____

_____

_____

_____

_____

_____

_____

_____

_____

_____

_____

_____

_____

_____

5-minute journaling:
Today I am grateful for...

_____

_____

_____

_____

_____

_____

_____

_____

_____

_____

_____

_____

_____

_____

_____

_____

_____

_____

_____

_____

5-minute journaling:
Today I am grateful for...

_____

_____

_____

_____

_____

_____

_____

_____

_____

_____

_____

_____

_____

_____

_____

_____

_____

_____

_____

_____

Weekly Planner

WEEK OF :

MONTH :

MONDAY

TUESDAY

WEDNESDAY

THURSDAY

FRIDAY

SATURDAY

NOTE :

QUOTE :

ORGANIZING MY THOUGHTS, MANIFESTING MY GOALS 2026

5-minute journaling:
Today I am grateful for...

_____

_____

_____

_____

_____

_____

_____

_____

_____

_____

_____

_____

_____

_____

_____

_____

_____

_____

_____

_____

5-minute journaling:
Today I am grateful for...

_____

_____

_____

_____

_____

_____

_____

_____

_____

_____

_____

_____

_____

_____

_____

_____

_____

_____

_____

5-minute journaling:
Today I am grateful for...

_____
_____
_____
_____
_____
_____
_____
_____
_____
_____
_____
_____
_____
_____
_____
_____
_____
_____
_____
_____

5-minute journaling:
Today I am grateful for...

_____
_____
_____
_____
_____
_____
_____
_____
_____
_____
_____
_____
_____
_____
_____
_____
_____
_____
_____
_____

5-minute journaling:
Today I am grateful for...

_____

_____

_____

_____

_____

_____

_____

_____

_____

_____

_____

_____

_____

_____

_____

_____

_____

_____

_____

_____

5-minute journaling:
Today I am grateful for...

_____

_____

_____

_____

_____

_____

_____

_____

_____

_____

_____

_____

_____

_____

_____

_____

_____

_____

MILESTONE ACCOMPLISHMENT

1) What did I accomplish:

_____

_____

2) When did I accomplish it:

_____

3) How did you accomplish it:

_____

_____

_____

4) What motivated you to accomplish it:

_____

_____

_____

5) Did you face any challenges while accomplishing it:

_____

_____

_____

6) How will you celebrate your accomplishment:

_____

_____

_____

What's On Your Mind?

★ _____

★ _____

★ _____

Month **AUGUST 2026**

Ideas, Tasks, Chores, Wishes, Dreams, Desires

➤ _____

➤ _____

➤ _____

➤ _____

➤ _____

➤ _____

➤ _____

➤ _____

➤ _____

➤ _____

➤ _____

➤ _____

VISION ———————— BOARD

Start each month with clarity and purpose. Reflect, plan, manifest. This journal is designed to help you stay organized, set priorities, and achieve your goals.

(Month): _____

Health

Career & Finances

Relationships & Social Life

Travel

Fitness

Spirituality & Mindfulness

Monthly goals

HEALTH GOALS

- ♡ _____
- ♡ _____
- ♡ _____

CAREER AND WORK GOALS

- ♡ _____
- ♡ _____
- ♡ _____

FITNESS GOALS

- ♡ _____
- ♡ _____
- ♡ _____

ORGANIZING MY THOUGHTS, MANIFESTING MY GOALS 2026

Monthly goals

RELATIONSHIP & SOCIAL LIFE GOALS

♡ _____
_____

♡ _____
_____

♡ _____
_____

TRAVEL GOALS

♡ _____
_____

♡ _____
_____

♡ _____
_____

SPIRITUAL AND MINDFULNESS GOALS

♡ _____
_____

♡ _____
_____

♡ _____
_____

Monthly goals

FINANCE GOALS

- ♡ _____
- ♡ _____
- ♡ _____

OTHER GOALS

- ♡ _____
- ♡ _____
- ♡ _____

OTHER GOALS

- ♡ _____
- ♡ _____
- ♡ _____

ORGANIZING MY THOUGHTS, MANIFESTING MY GOALS 2026

Weekly Planner

WEEK OF :

MONTH :

MONDAY

TUESDAY

WEDNESDAY

THURSDAY

FRIDAY

SATURDAY

NOTE :

QUOTE :

ORGANIZING MY THOUGHTS, MANIFESTING MY GOALS 2026

5-minute journaling:
Today I am grateful for...

_____

_____

_____

_____

_____

_____

_____

_____

_____

_____

_____

_____

_____

_____

_____

_____

_____

_____

_____

5-minute journaling:
Today I am grateful for...

_____
_____
_____
_____
_____
_____
_____
_____
_____
_____
_____
_____
_____
_____
_____
_____
_____
_____
_____
_____
_____

5-minute journaling:
Today I am grateful for...

_____

_____

_____

_____

_____

_____

_____

_____

_____

_____

_____

_____

_____

_____

_____

_____

_____

_____

_____

_____

_____

5-minute journaling:
Today I am grateful for...

_____

_____

_____

_____

_____

_____

_____

_____

_____

_____

_____

_____

_____

_____

_____

_____

_____

_____

_____

_____

5-minute journaling:
Today I am grateful for...

_____

_____

_____

_____

_____

_____

_____

_____

_____

_____

_____

_____

_____

_____

_____

_____

_____

_____

_____

5-minute journaling:
Today I am grateful for...

_____

_____

_____

_____

_____

_____

_____

_____

_____

_____

_____

_____

_____

_____

_____

_____

_____

_____

_____

_____

_____

5-minute journaling:
Today I am grateful for...

_____

_____

_____

_____

_____

_____

_____

_____

_____

_____

_____

_____

_____

_____

_____

_____

_____

_____

_____

5-minute journaling:
Today I am grateful for...

_____

_____

_____

_____

_____

_____

_____

_____

_____

_____

_____

_____

_____

_____

_____

_____

_____

_____

_____

_____

Weekly Planner

WEEK OF :

MONTH :

MONDAY

TUESDAY

WEDNESDAY

THURSDAY

FRIDAY

SATURDAY

NOTE :

QUOTE :

ORGANIZING MY THOUGHTS, MANIFESTING MY GOALS 2026

5-minute journaling:
Today I am grateful for...

_____

_____

_____

_____

_____

_____

_____

_____

_____

_____

_____

_____

_____

_____

_____

_____

_____

_____

_____

_____

5-minute journaling:
Today I am grateful for...

_____
_____
_____
_____
_____
_____
_____
_____
_____
_____
_____
_____
_____
_____
_____
_____
_____
_____

5-minute journaling:
Today I am grateful for...

_____

_____

_____

_____

_____

_____

_____

_____

_____

_____

_____

_____

_____

_____

_____

_____

_____

_____

_____

5-minute journaling:
Today I am grateful for...

_____

_____

_____

_____

_____

_____

_____

_____

_____

_____

_____

_____

_____

_____

_____

_____

_____

_____

_____

5-minute journaling:
Today I am grateful for...

_____

_____

_____

_____

_____

_____

_____

_____

_____

_____

_____

_____

_____

_____

_____

_____

_____

_____

_____

5-minute journaling:
Today I am grateful for...

_____
_____
_____
_____
_____
_____
_____
_____
_____
_____
_____
_____
_____
_____
_____
_____
_____
_____

5-minute journaling:
Today I am grateful for...

_____

_____

_____

_____

_____

_____

_____

_____

_____

_____

_____

_____

_____

_____

_____

_____

_____

_____

_____

_____

Weekly Planner

WEEK OF :

MONTH :

MONDAY

TUESDAY

WEDNESDAY

THURSDAY

FRIDAY

SATURDAY

NOTE :

QUOTE :

ORGANIZING MY THOUGHTS, MANIFESTING MY GOALS 2026

5-minute journaling:
Today I am grateful for...

_____

_____

_____

_____

_____

_____

_____

_____

_____

_____

_____

_____

_____

_____

_____

_____

_____

_____

_____

_____

5-minute journaling:
Today I am grateful for...

_____
_____
_____
_____
_____
_____
_____
_____
_____
_____
_____
_____
_____
_____
_____
_____
_____
_____
_____

5-minute journaling:
Today I am grateful for...

_____

_____

_____

_____

_____

_____

_____

_____

_____

_____

_____

_____

_____

_____

_____

_____

_____

_____

_____

_____

_____

5-minute journaling:
Today I am grateful for...

_____
_____
_____
_____
_____
_____
_____
_____
_____
_____
_____
_____
_____
_____
_____
_____
_____
_____
_____

5-minute journaling:
Today I am grateful for...

_____

_____

_____

_____

_____

_____

_____

_____

_____

_____

_____

_____

_____

_____

_____

_____

_____

_____

_____

5-minute journaling:
Today I am grateful for...

_____
_____
_____
_____
_____
_____
_____
_____
_____
_____
_____
_____
_____
_____
_____
_____
_____
_____
_____
_____

5-minute journaling:
Today I am grateful for...

_____

_____

_____

_____

_____

_____

_____

_____

_____

_____

_____

_____

_____

_____

_____

_____

_____

_____

_____

_____

Weekly Planner

WEEK OF :

MONTH :

MONDAY

TUESDAY

WEDNESDAY

THURSDAY

FRIDAY

SATURDAY

NOTE :

QUOTE :

ORGANIZING MY THOUGHTS, MANIFESTING MY GOALS 2026

5-minute journaling:
Today I am grateful for...

_____

_____

_____

_____

_____

_____

_____

_____

_____

_____

_____

_____

_____

_____

_____

_____

_____

_____

_____

_____

_____

_____

5-minute journaling:
Today I am grateful for...

_____

_____

_____

_____

_____

_____

_____

_____

_____

_____

_____

_____

_____

_____

_____

_____

_____

_____

_____

5-minute journaling:
Today I am grateful for...

_____

_____

_____

_____

_____

_____

_____

_____

_____

_____

_____

_____

_____

_____

_____

_____

_____

_____

_____

_____

_____

5-minute journaling:
Today I am grateful for...

_____

_____

_____

_____

_____

_____

_____

_____

_____

_____

_____

_____

_____

_____

_____

_____

_____

_____

_____

_____

5-minute journaling:
Today I am grateful for...

_____

_____

_____

_____

_____

_____

_____

_____

_____

_____

_____

_____

_____

_____

_____

_____

_____

_____

_____

_____

5-minute journaling:
Today I am grateful for...

_____

_____

_____

_____

_____

_____

_____

_____

_____

_____

_____

_____

_____

_____

_____

_____

_____

_____

_____

_____

5-minute journaling:
Today I am grateful for...

_____

_____

_____

_____

_____

_____

_____

_____

_____

_____

_____

_____

_____

_____

_____

_____

_____

_____

_____

_____

_____

Weekly Planner

WEEK OF :

MONTH :

MONDAY

TUESDAY

WEDNESDAY

THURSDAY

FRIDAY

SATURDAY

NOTE :

QUOTE :

ORGANIZING MY THOUGHTS, MANIFESTING MY GOALS 2026

5-minute journaling:
Today I am grateful for...

_____

_____

_____

_____

_____

_____

_____

_____

_____

_____

_____

_____

_____

_____

_____

_____

_____

_____

_____

_____

_____

5-minute journaling:
Today I am grateful for...

_____
_____
_____
_____
_____
_____
_____
_____
_____
_____
_____
_____
_____
_____
_____
_____
_____
_____
_____
_____

MILESTONE ACCOMPLISHMENT

1) What did I accomplish:

_____

_____

2) When did I accomplish it:

_____

3) How did you accomplish it:

_____

_____

_____

4) What motivated you to accomplish it:

_____

_____

_____

5) Did you face any challenges while accomplishing it:

_____

_____

_____

6) How will you celebrate your accomplishment:

_____

_____

_____

What's On Your Mind?

★ _____

★ _____

★ _____

Month **SEPTEMBER 2026**

Ideas, Tasks, Chores, Wishes, Dreams, Desires

➤ _____

➤ _____

➤ _____

➤ _____

➤ _____

➤ _____

➤ _____

➤ _____

➤ _____

➤ _____

➤ _____

➤ _____

➤ _____

VISION —————— BOARD

Start each month with clarity and purpose. Reflect, plan, manifest. This journal is designed to help you stay organized, set priorities, and achieve your goals.

(Month): _____

Health

Career & Finances

Relationships & Social Life

Travel

Fitness

Spirituality & Mindfulness

Monthly goals

HEALTH GOALS

- ♡ _____
- ♡ _____
- ♡ _____

CAREER AND WORK GOALS

- ♡ _____
- ♡ _____
- ♡ _____

FITNESS GOALS

- ♡ _____
- ♡ _____
- ♡ _____

Monthly goals

RELATIONSHIP & SOCIAL LIFE GOALS

♡ _____
♡ _____
♡ _____

TRAVEL GOALS

♡ _____
♡ _____
♡ _____

SPIRITUAL AND MINDFULNESS GOALS

♡ _____
♡ _____
♡ _____

Monthly goals

FINANCE GOALS

♡ _____

♡ _____

♡ _____

OTHER GOALS

♡ _____

♡ _____

♡ _____

OTHER GOALS

♡ _____

♡ _____

♡ _____

Weekly Planner

WEEK OF :

MONTH :

MONDAY

TUESDAY

WEDNESDAY

THURSDAY

FRIDAY

SATURDAY

NOTE :

QUOTE :

ORGANIZING MY THOUGHTS, MANIFESTING MY GOALS 2026

5-minute journaling:
Today I am grateful for...

_____
_____
_____
_____
_____
_____
_____
_____
_____
_____
_____
_____
_____
_____
_____
_____
_____
_____

5-minute journaling:
Today I am grateful for...

_____

_____

_____

_____

_____

_____

_____

_____

_____

_____

_____

_____

_____

_____

_____

_____

_____

_____

_____

_____

5-minute journaling:
Today I am grateful for...

_____

_____

_____

_____

_____

_____

_____

_____

_____

_____

_____

_____

_____

_____

_____

_____

_____

_____

_____

_____

5-minute journaling:
Today I am grateful for...

_____

_____

_____

_____

_____

_____

_____

_____

_____

_____

_____

_____

_____

_____

_____

_____

_____

_____

_____

_____

_____

5-minute journaling:
Today I am grateful for...

_____

_____

_____

_____

_____

_____

_____

_____

_____

_____

_____

_____

_____

_____

_____

_____

_____

_____

_____

_____

Weekly Planner

MONDAY

TUESDAY

WEDNESDAY

THURSDAY

FRIDAY

SATURDAY

NOTE :

QUOTE :

ORGANIZING MY THOUGHTS, MANIFESTING MY GOALS 2026

5-minute journaling:
Today I am grateful for...

_____
_____
_____
_____
_____
_____
_____
_____
_____
_____
_____
_____
_____
_____
_____
_____
_____
_____
_____
_____

5-minute journaling:
Today I am grateful for...

_____
_____
_____
_____
_____
_____
_____
_____
_____
_____
_____
_____
_____
_____
_____
_____
_____
_____
_____
_____

5-minute journaling:
Today I am grateful for...

_____
_____
_____
_____
_____
_____
_____
_____
_____
_____
_____
_____
_____
_____
_____
_____
_____
_____
_____

5-minute journaling:
Today I am grateful for...

_____

_____

_____

_____

_____

_____

_____

_____

_____

_____

_____

_____

_____

_____

_____

_____

_____

_____

_____

5-minute journaling:
Today I am grateful for...

_____

_____

_____

_____

_____

_____

_____

_____

_____

_____

_____

_____

_____

_____

_____

_____

_____

_____

_____

5-minute journaling:
Today I am grateful for...

_____

_____

_____

_____

_____

_____

_____

_____

_____

_____

_____

_____

_____

_____

_____

_____

_____

_____

_____

5-minute journaling:
Today I am grateful for...

_____
_____
_____
_____
_____
_____
_____
_____
_____
_____
_____
_____
_____
_____
_____
_____
_____
_____
_____

Weekly Planner

WEEK OF :

MONTH :

MONDAY

TUESDAY

WEDNESDAY

THURSDAY

FRIDAY

SATURDAY

NOTE :

QUOTE :

ORGANIZING MY THOUGHTS, MANIFESTING MY GOALS 2026

5-minute journaling:
Today I am grateful for...

_____

_____

_____

_____

_____

_____

_____

_____

_____

_____

_____

_____

_____

_____

_____

_____

_____

_____

_____

_____

5-minute journaling:
Today I am grateful for...

_____

_____

_____

_____

_____

_____

_____

_____

_____

_____

_____

_____

_____

_____

_____

_____

_____

_____

_____

_____

_____

5-minute journaling:
Today I am grateful for...

_____

_____

_____

_____

_____

_____

_____

_____

_____

_____

_____

_____

_____

_____

_____

_____

_____

_____

_____

5-minute journaling:
Today I am grateful for...

_____

_____

_____

_____

_____

_____

_____

_____

_____

_____

_____

_____

_____

_____

_____

_____

_____

_____

_____

5-minute journaling:
Today I am grateful for...

_____

_____

_____

_____

_____

_____

_____

_____

_____

_____

_____

_____

_____

_____

_____

_____

_____

_____

_____

_____

5-minute journaling:
Today I am grateful for...

_____

_____

_____

_____

_____

_____

_____

_____

_____

_____

_____

_____

_____

_____

_____

_____

_____

_____

_____

_____

_____

5-minute journaling:
Today I am grateful for...

_____

_____

_____

_____

_____

_____

_____

_____

_____

_____

_____

_____

_____

_____

_____

_____

_____

_____

_____

_____

Weekly Planner

MONDAY

TUESDAY

WEDNESDAY

THURSDAY

FRIDAY

SATURDAY

NOTE :

QUOTE :

ORGANIZING MY THOUGHTS, MANIFESTING MY GOALS 2026

5-minute journaling:
Today I am grateful for...

_____
_____
_____
_____
_____
_____
_____
_____
_____
_____
_____
_____
_____
_____
_____
_____
_____
_____
_____
_____
_____

5-minute journaling:
Today I am grateful for...

_____
_____
_____
_____
_____
_____
_____
_____
_____
_____
_____
_____
_____
_____
_____
_____
_____
_____
_____

5-minute journaling:
Today I am grateful for...

_____
_____
_____
_____
_____
_____
_____
_____
_____
_____
_____
_____
_____
_____
_____
_____
_____
_____
_____
_____
_____

5-minute journaling:
Today I am grateful for...

_____
_____
_____
_____
_____
_____
_____
_____
_____
_____
_____
_____
_____
_____
_____
_____
_____
_____
_____
_____
_____

5-minute journaling:
Today I am grateful for...

_____

_____

_____

_____

_____

_____

_____

_____

_____

_____

_____

_____

_____

_____

_____

_____

_____

_____

_____

_____

5-minute journaling:
Today I am grateful for...

_____

_____

_____

_____

_____

_____

_____

_____

_____

_____

_____

_____

_____

_____

_____

_____

_____

_____

_____

5-minute journaling:
Today I am grateful for...

Weekly Planner

WEEK OF :

MONTH :

MONDAY

TUESDAY

WEDNESDAY

THURSDAY

FRIDAY

SATURDAY

NOTE :

QUOTE :

ORGANIZING MY THOUGHTS, MANIFESTING MY GOALS 2026

5-minute journaling:
Today I am grateful for...

_____

_____

_____

_____

_____

_____

_____

_____

_____

_____

_____

_____

_____

_____

_____

_____

_____

_____

_____

_____

5-minute journaling:
Today I am grateful for...

_____

_____

_____

_____

_____

_____

_____

_____

_____

_____

_____

_____

_____

_____

_____

_____

_____

_____

_____

_____

5-minute journaling:
Today I am grateful for...

_____
_____
_____
_____
_____
_____
_____
_____
_____
_____
_____
_____
_____
_____
_____
_____
_____
_____
_____
_____
_____

5-minute journaling:
Today I am grateful for...

_____

_____

_____

_____

_____

_____

_____

_____

_____

_____

_____

_____

_____

_____

_____

_____

_____

_____

_____

_____

MILESTONE ACCOMPLISHMENT

1) What did I accomplish:

_____

_____

2) When did I accomplish it: _____

3) How did you accomplish it:

_____

_____

_____

4) What motivated you to accomplish it:

_____

_____

_____

5) Did you face any challenges while accomplishing it:

_____

_____

_____

6) How will you celebrate your accomplishment:

_____

_____

_____

What's On Your Mind?

★ _____

★ _____

★ _____

Month **OCTOBER 2026**

Ideas, Tasks, Chores, Wishes, Dreams, Desires

➤ _____

➤ _____

➤ _____

➤ _____

➤ _____

➤ _____

➤ _____

➤ _____

➤ _____

➤ _____

➤ _____

➤ _____

VISION ———————— BOARD

Start each month with clarity and purpose. Reflect, plan, manifest. This journal is designed to help you stay organized, set priorities, and achieve your goals.

(Month): _____

Health

Career & Finances

Relationships & Social Life

Travel

Fitness

Spirituality & Mindfulness

Monthly goals

HEALTH GOALS

♡ _____

♡ _____

♡ _____

CAREER AND WORK GOALS

♡ _____

♡ _____

♡ _____

FITNESS GOALS

♡ _____

♡ _____

♡ _____

Monthly goals

RELATIONSHIP & SOCIAL LIFE GOALS

♡ _____

♡ _____

♡ _____

TRAVEL GOALS

♡ _____

♡ _____

♡ _____

SPIRITUAL AND MINDFULNESS GOALS

♡ _____

♡ _____

♡ _____

Monthly goals

FINANCE GOALS

- ♡ _____
- ♡ _____
- ♡ _____

OTHER GOALS

- ♡ _____
- ♡ _____
- ♡ _____

OTHER GOALS

- ♡ _____
- ♡ _____
- ♡ _____

ORGANIZING MY THOUGHTS, MANIFESTING MY GOALS 2026

Weekly Planner

WEEK OF :

MONTH :

MONDAY

TUESDAY

WEDNESDAY

THURSDAY

FRIDAY

SATURDAY

NOTE :

QUOTE :

ORGANIZING MY THOUGHTS, MANIFESTING MY GOALS 2026

5-minute journaling:
Today I am grateful for...

_____

_____

_____

_____

_____

_____

_____

_____

_____

_____

_____

_____

_____

_____

_____

_____

_____

_____

_____

_____

_____

5-minute journaling:
Today I am grateful for...

_____

_____

_____

_____

_____

_____

_____

_____

_____

_____

_____

_____

_____

_____

_____

_____

_____

_____

_____

5-minute journaling:
Today I am grateful for...

_____

_____

_____

_____

_____

_____

_____

_____

_____

_____

_____

_____

_____

_____

_____

_____

_____

_____

_____

Weekly Planner

WEEK OF :

MONTH :

MONDAY

TUESDAY

WEDNESDAY

THURSDAY

FRIDAY

SATURDAY

NOTE :

QUOTE :

ORGANIZING MY THOUGHTS, MANIFESTING MY GOALS 2026

5-minute journaling:
Today I am grateful for...

_____

_____

_____

_____

_____

_____

_____

_____

_____

_____

_____

_____

_____

_____

_____

_____

_____

_____

5-minute journaling:
Today I am grateful for...

_____

_____

_____

_____

_____

_____

_____

_____

_____

_____

_____

_____

_____

_____

_____

_____

_____

_____

_____

_____

5-minute journaling:
Today I am grateful for...

_____

_____

_____

_____

_____

_____

_____

_____

_____

_____

_____

_____

_____

_____

_____

_____

_____

_____

5-minute journaling:
Today I am grateful for...

_____

_____

_____

_____

_____

_____

_____

_____

_____

_____

_____

_____

_____

_____

_____

_____

_____

_____

_____

_____

_____

5-minute journaling:
Today I am grateful for...

_____

_____

_____

_____

_____

_____

_____

_____

_____

_____

_____

_____

_____

_____

_____

_____

_____

_____

_____

5-minute journaling:
Today I am grateful for...

_____
_____
_____
_____
_____
_____
_____
_____
_____
_____
_____
_____
_____
_____
_____
_____
_____
_____
_____
_____
_____

5-minute journaling:
Today I am grateful for...

_____

_____

_____

_____

_____

_____

_____

_____

_____

_____

_____

_____

_____

_____

_____

_____

_____

_____

_____

_____

Weekly Planner

WEEK OF :

MONTH :

MONDAY

TUESDAY

WEDNESDAY

THURSDAY

FRIDAY

SATURDAY

NOTE :

QUOTE :

ORGANIZING MY THOUGHTS, MANIFESTING MY GOALS 2026

5-minute journaling:
Today I am grateful for...

_____

_____

_____

_____

_____

_____

_____

_____

_____

_____

_____

_____

_____

_____

_____

_____

_____

_____

_____

5-minute journaling:
Today I am grateful for...

_____
_____
_____
_____
_____
_____
_____
_____
_____
_____
_____
_____
_____
_____
_____
_____
_____
_____
_____

5-minute journaling:
Today I am grateful for...

_____
_____
_____
_____
_____
_____
_____
_____
_____
_____
_____
_____
_____
_____
_____
_____
_____
_____
_____
_____

5-minute journaling:
Today I am grateful for...

_____

_____

_____

_____

_____

_____

_____

_____

_____

_____

_____

_____

_____

_____

_____

_____

_____

_____

_____

_____

5-minute journaling:
Today I am grateful for...

_____

_____

_____

_____

_____

_____

_____

_____

_____

_____

_____

_____

_____

_____

_____

_____

_____

_____

_____

_____

5-minute journaling:
Today I am grateful for...

_____

_____

_____

_____

_____

_____

_____

_____

_____

_____

_____

_____

_____

_____

_____

_____

_____

_____

_____

_____

_____

_____

5-minute journaling:
Today I am grateful for...

_____

_____

_____

_____

_____

_____

_____

_____

_____

_____

_____

_____

_____

_____

_____

_____

_____

_____

_____

Weekly Planner

WEEK OF :

MONTH :

MONDAY

TUESDAY

WEDNESDAY

THURSDAY

FRIDAY

SATURDAY

NOTE :

QUOTE :

ORGANIZING MY THOUGHTS, MANIFESTING MY GOALS 2026

5-minute journaling:
Today I am grateful for...

_____

_____

_____

_____

_____

_____

_____

_____

_____

_____

_____

_____

_____

_____

_____

_____

_____

_____

_____

5-minute journaling:
Today I am grateful for...

_____

_____

_____

_____

_____

_____

_____

_____

_____

_____

_____

_____

_____

_____

_____

_____

_____

_____

_____

_____

_____

5-minute journaling:
Today I am grateful for...

_____

_____

_____

_____

_____

_____

_____

_____

_____

_____

_____

_____

_____

_____

_____

_____

_____

_____

_____

_____

_____

5-minute journaling:
Today I am grateful for...

_____
_____
_____
_____
_____
_____
_____
_____
_____
_____
_____
_____
_____
_____
_____
_____
_____
_____
_____

5-minute journaling:
Today I am grateful for...

_____

_____

_____

_____

_____

_____

_____

_____

_____

_____

_____

_____

_____

_____

_____

_____

_____

_____

_____

_____

_____

_____

5-minute journaling:
Today I am grateful for...

_____

_____

_____

_____

_____

_____

_____

_____

_____

_____

_____

_____

_____

_____

_____

_____

_____

_____

_____

5-minute journaling:
Today I am grateful for...

_____

_____

_____

_____

_____

_____

_____

_____

_____

_____

_____

_____

_____

_____

_____

_____

_____

_____

_____

Weekly Planner

WEEK OF :

MONTH :

MONDAY

TUESDAY

WEDNESDAY

THURSDAY

FRIDAY

SATURDAY

NOTE :

QUOTE :

ORGANIZING MY THOUGHTS, MANIFESTING MY GOALS 2026

5-minute journaling:
Today I am grateful for...

_____

_____

_____

_____

_____

_____

_____

_____

_____

_____

_____

_____

_____

_____

_____

_____

_____

_____

_____

_____

5-minute journaling:
Today I am grateful for...

_____
_____
_____
_____
_____
_____
_____
_____
_____
_____
_____
_____
_____
_____
_____
_____
_____
_____
_____
_____

5-minute journaling:
Today I am grateful for...

_____

_____

_____

_____

_____

_____

_____

_____

_____

_____

_____

_____

_____

_____

_____

_____

_____

_____

_____

5-minute journaling:
Today I am grateful for...

_____

_____

_____

_____

_____

_____

_____

_____

_____

_____

_____

_____

_____

_____

_____

_____

_____

_____

_____

_____

5-minute journaling:
Today I am grateful for...

_____

_____

_____

_____

_____

_____

_____

_____

_____

_____

_____

_____

_____

_____

_____

_____

_____

_____

_____

5-minute journaling:
Today I am grateful for...

_____
_____
_____
_____
_____
_____
_____
_____
_____
_____
_____
_____
_____
_____
_____
_____
_____
_____
_____
_____
_____

5-minute journaling:
Today I am grateful for...

_____

_____

_____

_____

_____

_____

_____

_____

_____

_____

_____

_____

_____

_____

_____

_____

_____

_____

_____

MILESTONE ACCOMPLISHMENT

1) What did I accomplish:

_____

_____

2) When did I accomplish it:

_____

3) How did you accomplish it:

_____

_____

_____

4) What motivated you to accomplish it:

_____

_____

_____

5) Did you face any challenges while accomplishing it:

_____

_____

_____

6) How will you celebrate your accomplishment:

_____

_____

_____

What's On Your Mind?

★ _____

★ _____

★ _____

Month **NOVEMBER 2026**

Ideas, Tasks, Chores, Wishes, Dreams, Desires

➤ _____

➤ _____

➤ _____

➤ _____

➤ _____

➤ _____

➤ _____

➤ _____

➤ _____

➤ _____

➤ _____

➤ _____

VISION ———————— BOARD

Start each month with clarity and purpose. Reflect, plan, manifest. This journal is designed to help you stay organized, set priorities, and achieve your goals.

(Month): _____

Health

Career & Finances

Relationships & Social Life

Travel

Fitness

Spirituality & Mindfulness

Monthly goals

HEALTH GOALS

♡ _____

♡ _____

♡ _____

CAREER AND WORK GOALS

♡ _____

♡ _____

♡ _____

FITNESS GOALS

♡ _____

♡ _____

♡ _____

Monthly goals

RELATIONSHIP & SOCIAL LIFE GOALS

- ♡ _____
- ♡ _____
- ♡ _____

TRAVEL GOALS

- ♡ _____
- ♡ _____
- ♡ _____

SPIRITUAL AND MINDFULNESS GOALS

- ♡ _____
- ♡ _____
- ♡ _____

Monthly goals

FINANCE GOALS

- ♡ _____
- ♡ _____
- ♡ _____

OTHER GOALS

- ♡ _____
- ♡ _____
- ♡ _____

OTHER GOALS

- ♡ _____
- ♡ _____
- ♡ _____

Weekly Planner

WEEK OF :

MONTH :

MONDAY

TUESDAY

WEDNESDAY

THURSDAY

FRIDAY

SATURDAY

NOTE :

QUOTE :

ORGANIZING MY THOUGHTS, MANIFESTING MY GOALS 2026

5-minute journaling:
Today I am grateful for...

_____

_____

_____

_____

_____

_____

_____

_____

_____

_____

_____

_____

_____

_____

_____

_____

_____

_____

_____

5-minute journaling:
Today I am grateful for...

_____
_____
_____
_____
_____
_____
_____
_____
_____
_____
_____
_____
_____
_____
_____
_____
_____
_____
_____

5-minute journaling:
Today I am grateful for...

_____

_____

_____

_____

_____

_____

_____

_____

_____

_____

_____

_____

_____

_____

_____

_____

_____

_____

_____

_____

_____

5-minute journaling:
Today I am grateful for...

_____

_____

_____

_____

_____

_____

_____

_____

_____

_____

_____

_____

_____

_____

_____

_____

_____

_____

_____

5-minute journaling:
Today I am grateful for...

_____

_____

_____

_____

_____

_____

_____

_____

_____

_____

_____

_____

_____

_____

_____

_____

_____

_____

_____

5-minute journaling:
Today I am grateful for...

_____

_____

_____

_____

_____

_____

_____

_____

_____

_____

_____

_____

_____

_____

_____

_____

_____

_____

5-minute journaling:
Today I am grateful for...

_____

_____

_____

_____

_____

_____

_____

_____

_____

_____

_____

_____

_____

_____

_____

_____

_____

_____

_____

Weekly Planner

WEEK OF :

MONTH :

MONDAY

TUESDAY

WEDNESDAY

THURSDAY

FRIDAY

SATURDAY

NOTE :

QUOTE :

ORGANIZING MY THOUGHTS, MANIFESTING MY GOALS 2026

5-minute journaling:
Today I am grateful for...

_____

_____

_____

_____

_____

_____

_____

_____

_____

_____

_____

_____

_____

_____

_____

_____

_____

_____

_____

5-minute journaling:
Today I am grateful for...

_____

_____

_____

_____

_____

_____

_____

_____

_____

_____

_____

_____

_____

_____

_____

_____

_____

_____

_____

_____

_____

_____

5-minute journaling:
Today I am grateful for...

_____

_____

_____

_____

_____

_____

_____

_____

_____

_____

_____

_____

_____

_____

_____

_____

_____

_____

_____

5-minute journaling:
Today I am grateful for...

_____

_____

_____

_____

_____

_____

_____

_____

_____

_____

_____

_____

_____

_____

_____

_____

_____

_____

_____

_____

5-minute journaling:
Today I am grateful for...

_____

_____

_____

_____

_____

_____

_____

_____

_____

_____

_____

_____

_____

_____

_____

_____

_____

_____

_____

_____

_____

5-minute journaling:
Today I am grateful for...

_____

_____

_____

_____

_____

_____

_____

_____

_____

_____

_____

_____

_____

_____

_____

_____

_____

_____

_____

5-minute journaling:
Today I am grateful for...

_____

_____

_____

_____

_____

_____

_____

_____

_____

_____

_____

_____

_____

_____

_____

_____

_____

_____

Weekly Planner

WEEK OF :

MONTH :

MONDAY

TUESDAY

WEDNESDAY

THURSDAY

FRIDAY

SATURDAY

NOTE :

QUOTE :

ORGANIZING MY THOUGHTS, MANIFESTING MY GOALS 2026

5-minute journaling:
Today I am grateful for...

_____

_____

_____

_____

_____

_____

_____

_____

_____

_____

_____

_____

_____

_____

_____

_____

_____

_____

_____

5-minute journaling:
Today I am grateful for...

_____
_____
_____
_____
_____
_____
_____
_____
_____
_____
_____
_____
_____
_____
_____
_____
_____
_____
_____
_____
_____

5-minute journaling:
Today I am grateful for...

_____

_____

_____

_____

_____

_____

_____

_____

_____

_____

_____

_____

_____

_____

_____

_____

_____

_____

_____

_____

_____

5-minute journaling:
Today I am grateful for...

_____
_____
_____
_____
_____
_____
_____
_____
_____
_____
_____
_____
_____
_____
_____
_____
_____
_____
_____

5-minute journaling:
Today I am grateful for...

_____

_____

_____

_____

_____

_____

_____

_____

_____

_____

_____

_____

_____

_____

_____

_____

_____

_____

5-minute journaling:
Today I am grateful for...

_____

_____

_____

_____

_____

_____

_____

_____

_____

_____

_____

_____

_____

_____

_____

_____

_____

_____

_____

5-minute journaling:
Today I am grateful for...

_____

_____

_____

_____

_____

_____

_____

_____

_____

_____

_____

_____

_____

_____

_____

_____

_____

_____

Weekly Planner

WEEK OF :

MONTH :

MONDAY

TUESDAY

WEDNESDAY

THURSDAY

FRIDAY

SATURDAY

NOTE :

QUOTE :

ORGANIZING MY THOUGHTS, MANIFESTING MY GOALS 2026

5-minute journaling:
Today I am grateful for...

_____

_____

_____

_____

_____

_____

_____

_____

_____

_____

_____

_____

_____

_____

_____

_____

_____

_____

_____

5-minute journaling:
Today I am grateful for...

_____
_____
_____
_____
_____
_____
_____
_____
_____
_____
_____
_____
_____
_____
_____
_____
_____
_____
_____
_____

5-minute journaling:
Today I am grateful for...

_____

_____

_____

_____

_____

_____

_____

_____

_____

_____

_____

_____

_____

_____

_____

_____

_____

_____

5-minute journaling:
Today I am grateful for...

_____
_____
_____
_____
_____
_____
_____
_____
_____
_____
_____
_____
_____
_____
_____
_____
_____
_____
_____

5-minute journaling:
Today I am grateful for...

_____

_____

_____

_____

_____

_____

_____

_____

_____

_____

_____

_____

_____

_____

_____

_____

_____

_____

_____

_____

5-minute journaling:
Today I am grateful for...

_____
_____
_____
_____
_____
_____
_____
_____
_____
_____
_____
_____
_____
_____
_____
_____
_____
_____

5-minute journaling:
Today I am grateful for...

_____

_____

_____

_____

_____

_____

_____

_____

_____

_____

_____

_____

_____

_____

_____

_____

_____

_____

5-minute journaling:
Today I am grateful for...

_____
_____
_____
_____
_____
_____
_____
_____
_____
_____
_____
_____
_____
_____
_____
_____
_____
_____
_____
_____
_____

MILESTONE ACCOMPLISHMENT

1) What did I accomplish:

_____

_____

2) When did I accomplish it:

_____

3) How did you accomplish it:

_____

_____

_____

4) What motivated you to accomplish it:

_____

_____

_____

5) Did you face any challenges while accomplishing it:

_____

_____

_____

6) How will you celebrate your accomplishment:

_____

_____

_____

What's On Your Mind?

★ _____

★ _____

★ _____

Month **DECEMBER 2026**

Ideas, Tasks, Chores, Wishes, Dreams, Desires

➤ _____

➤ _____

➤ _____

➤ _____

➤ _____

➤ _____

➤ _____

➤ _____

➤ _____

➤ _____

➤ _____

➤ _____

VISION ——————— BOARD

Start each month with clarity and purpose. Reflect, plan, manifest. This journal is designed to help you stay organized, set priorities, and achieve your goals.

(Month): _____

Health

Career & Finances

Relationships & Social Life

Travel

Fitness

Spirituality & Mindfulness

Monthly goals

HEALTH GOALS

- ♡ _____
- ♡ _____
- ♡ _____

CAREER AND WORK GOALS

- ♡ _____
- ♡ _____
- ♡ _____

FITNESS GOALS

- ♡ _____
- ♡ _____
- ♡ _____

Monthly goals

RELATIONSHIP & SOCIAL LIFE GOALS

♡ _____
♡ _____
♡ _____

TRAVEL GOALS

♡ _____
♡ _____
♡ _____

SPIRITUAL AND MINDFULNESS GOALS

♡ _____
♡ _____
♡ _____

Monthly goals

FINANCE GOALS

- ♡ _____
- ♡ _____
- ♡ _____

OTHER GOALS

- ♡ _____
- ♡ _____
- ♡ _____

OTHER GOALS

- ♡ _____
- ♡ _____
- ♡ _____

Weekly Planner

WEEK OF :

MONTH :

MONDAY

TUESDAY

WEDNESDAY

THURSDAY

FRIDAY

SATURDAY

NOTE :

QUOTE :

ORGANIZING MY THOUGHTS, MANIFESTING MY GOALS 2026

5-minute journaling:
Today I am grateful for...

_____

_____

_____

_____

_____

_____

_____

_____

_____

_____

_____

_____

_____

_____

_____

_____

_____

_____

_____

5-minute journaling:
Today I am grateful for...

_____

_____

_____

_____

_____

_____

_____

_____

_____

_____

_____

_____

_____

_____

_____

_____

_____

_____

_____

_____

_____

_____

5-minute journaling:
Today I am grateful for...

_____

_____

_____

_____

_____

_____

_____

_____

_____

_____

_____

_____

_____

_____

_____

_____

_____

_____

_____

5-minute journaling:
Today I am grateful for...

_____

_____

_____

_____

_____

_____

_____

_____

_____

_____

_____

_____

_____

_____

_____

_____

_____

_____

_____

_____

5-minute journaling:
Today I am grateful for...

_____

_____

_____

_____

_____

_____

_____

_____

_____

_____

_____

_____

_____

_____

_____

_____

_____

_____

_____

Weekly Planner

WEEK OF :

MONTH :

MONDAY

TUESDAY

WEDNESDAY

THURSDAY

FRIDAY

SATURDAY

NOTE :

QUOTE :

ORGANIZING MY THOUGHTS, MANIFESTING MY GOALS 2026

5-minute journaling:
Today I am grateful for...

_____

_____

_____

_____

_____

_____

_____

_____

_____

_____

_____

_____

_____

_____

_____

_____

_____

_____

_____

_____

5-minute journaling:
Today I am grateful for...

_____

_____

_____

_____

_____

_____

_____

_____

_____

_____

_____

_____

_____

_____

_____

_____

_____

_____

_____

5-minute journaling:
Today I am grateful for...

_____
_____
_____
_____
_____
_____
_____
_____
_____
_____
_____
_____
_____
_____
_____
_____
_____
_____
_____
_____

5-minute journaling:
Today I am grateful for...

_____

_____

_____

_____

_____

_____

_____

_____

_____

_____

_____

_____

_____

_____

_____

_____

_____

_____

5-minute journaling:
Today I am grateful for...

_____
_____
_____
_____
_____
_____
_____
_____
_____
_____
_____
_____
_____
_____
_____
_____
_____
_____
_____
_____
_____

5-minute journaling:
Today I am grateful for...

_____

_____

_____

_____

_____

_____

_____

_____

_____

_____

_____

_____

_____

_____

_____

_____

_____

_____

5-minute journaling:
Today I am grateful for...

_____

_____

_____

_____

_____

_____

_____

_____

_____

_____

_____

_____

_____

_____

_____

_____

_____

_____

_____

_____

Weekly Planner

WEEK OF :

MONTH :

MONDAY

TUESDAY

WEDNESDAY

THURSDAY

FRIDAY

SATURDAY

NOTE :

QUOTE :

ORGANIZING MY THOUGHTS, MANIFESTING MY GOALS 2026

5-minute journaling:
Today I am grateful for...

_____

_____

_____

_____

_____

_____

_____

_____

_____

_____

_____

_____

_____

_____

_____

_____

_____

_____

_____

_____

_____

_____

5-minute journaling:
Today I am grateful for...

_____

_____

_____

_____

_____

_____

_____

_____

_____

_____

_____

_____

_____

_____

_____

_____

_____

_____

_____

5-minute journaling:
Today I am grateful for...

_____
_____
_____
_____
_____
_____
_____
_____
_____
_____
_____
_____
_____
_____
_____
_____
_____
_____
_____
_____
_____

5-minute journaling:
Today I am grateful for...

_____

_____

_____

_____

_____

_____

_____

_____

_____

_____

_____

_____

_____

_____

_____

_____

_____

_____

_____

_____

5-minute journaling:
Today I am grateful for...

_____

_____

_____

_____

_____

_____

_____

_____

_____

_____

_____

_____

_____

_____

_____

_____

_____

_____

_____

_____

5-minute journaling:
Today I am grateful for...

_____

_____

_____

_____

_____

_____

_____

_____

_____

_____

_____

_____

_____

_____

_____

_____

_____

_____

_____

5-minute journaling:
Today I am grateful for...

_____

_____

_____

_____

_____

_____

_____

_____

_____

_____

_____

_____

_____

_____

_____

_____

_____

_____

_____

_____

_____

Weekly Planner

WEEK OF :

MONTH :

MONDAY

TUESDAY

WEDNESDAY

THURSDAY

FRIDAY

SATURDAY

NOTE :

QUOTE :

5-minute journaling:
Today I am grateful for...

_____

_____

_____

_____

_____

_____

_____

_____

_____

_____

_____

_____

_____

_____

_____

_____

_____

_____

_____

_____

5-minute journaling:
Today I am grateful for...

_____

_____

_____

_____

_____

_____

_____

_____

_____

_____

_____

_____

_____

_____

_____

_____

_____

_____

_____

5-minute journaling:
Today I am grateful for...

_____
_____
_____
_____
_____
_____
_____
_____
_____
_____
_____
_____
_____
_____
_____
_____
_____
_____
_____
_____
_____

5-minute journaling:
Today I am grateful for...

_____

_____

_____

_____

_____

_____

_____

_____

_____

_____

_____

_____

_____

_____

_____

_____

_____

_____

_____

_____

5-minute journaling:
Today I am grateful for...

_____
_____
_____
_____
_____
_____
_____
_____
_____
_____
_____
_____
_____
_____
_____
_____
_____
_____
_____
_____
_____

5-minute journaling:
Today I am grateful for...

_____

_____

_____

_____

_____

_____

_____

_____

_____

_____

_____

_____

_____

_____

_____

_____

_____

_____

5-minute journaling:
Today I am grateful for...

_____

_____

_____

_____

_____

_____

_____

_____

_____

_____

_____

_____

_____

_____

_____

_____

_____

_____

_____

_____

_____

Weekly Planner

WEEK OF :

MONTH :

MONDAY

TUESDAY

WEDNESDAY

THURSDAY

FRIDAY

SATURDAY

NOTE :

QUOTE :

ORGANIZING MY THOUGHTS, MANIFESTING MY GOALS 2026

5-minute journaling:
Today I am grateful for...

_____
_____
_____
_____
_____
_____
_____
_____
_____
_____
_____
_____
_____
_____
_____
_____
_____
_____
_____
_____

5-minute journaling:
Today I am grateful for...

_____
_____
_____
_____
_____
_____
_____
_____
_____
_____
_____
_____
_____
_____
_____
_____
_____
_____
_____

5-minute journaling:
Today I am grateful for...

_____

_____

_____

_____

_____

_____

_____

_____

_____

_____

_____

_____

_____

_____

_____

_____

_____

_____

_____

_____

5-minute journaling:
Today I am grateful for...

_____
_____
_____
_____
_____
_____
_____
_____
_____
_____
_____
_____
_____
_____
_____
_____
_____
_____
_____
_____

5-minute journaling:
Today I am grateful for...

_____
_____
_____
_____
_____
_____
_____
_____
_____
_____
_____
_____
_____
_____
_____
_____
_____
_____
_____
_____
_____

MILESTONE ACCOMPLISHMENT

1) What did I accomplish:

_____

_____

2) When did I accomplish it:

_____

3) How did you accomplish it:

_____

_____

_____

4) What motivated you to accomplish it:

_____

_____

_____

5) Did you face any challenges while accomplishing it:

_____

_____

_____

6) How will you celebrate your accomplishment:

_____

_____

_____

www.ingramcontent.com/pod-product-compliance
Lightning Source LLC
Chambersburg PA
CBHW081527120626
46550CB00009B/2638